THE USBORNE
INTERNET-LINKED
WORLD ATLAS
OF
DINOSAURS

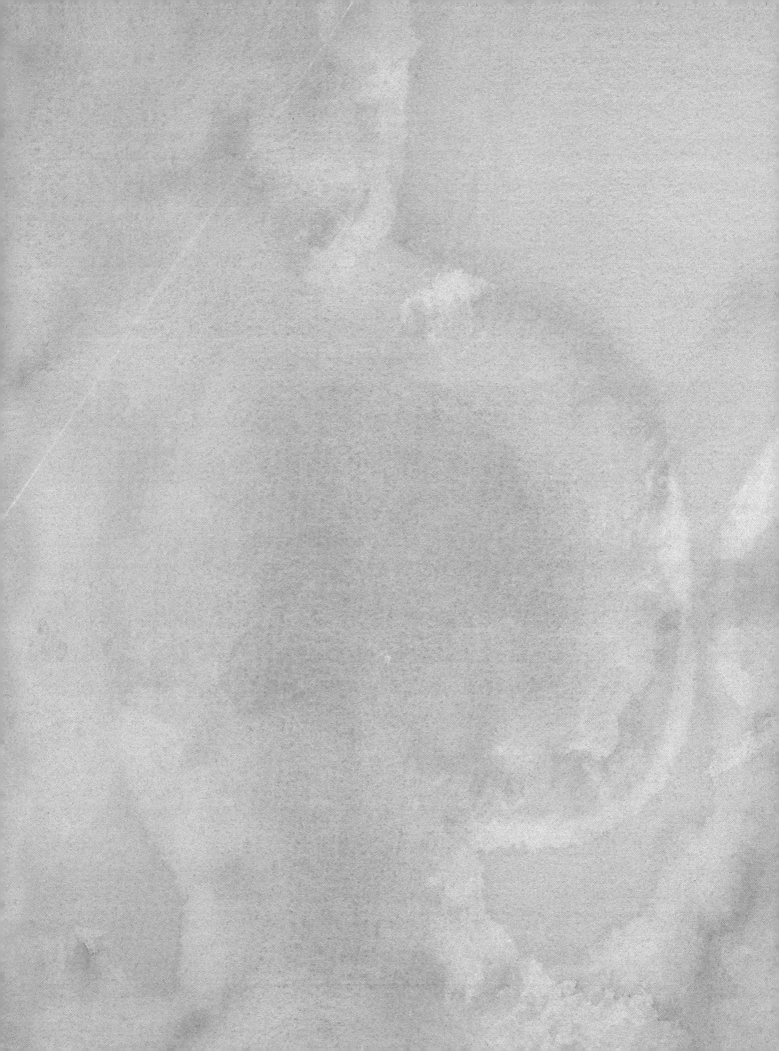

THE USBORNE
INTERNET - LINKED
WORLD ATLAS
OF
DINOSAURS

THE USBORNE
INTERNET-LINKED
WORLD ATLAS
OF
DINOSAURS

SCHOLASTIC INC.

New York Toronto London Auckland Sydney
Mexico City New Delhi Hong Kong Buenos Aires

Susanna Davidson,
Stephanie Turnbull and Rachel Firth

Designed by Andrea Slane,
Laura Parker, Nelupa Hussain and Glen Bird

Illustrated by Luis Rey, Todd Marshall,
Barry Croucher, Glen Bird and Ian Jackson
Consultants: Darren Naish and Dr. David Martill

Contents

Internet links

This book contains descriptions of many interesting websites where you can find out more about dinosaurs and the places where they have been found. For links to these sites, go to the Usborne Quicklinks Website at **www.usborne-quicklinks.com** and enter the keywords "atlas of dinosaurs". There you will find links to take you to all the websites.

Site availability

The links on the Usborne Quicklinks Website will be reviewed and updated regularly. If any sites become unavailable, we will, if possible, replace them with suitable alternatives.

Occasionally, you may get a message saying that a website is unavailable. This may be temporary, so try again a few hours later, or even the next day.

> **Internet link**
> For links to all the websites described in this book, go to www.usborne-quicklinks.com and enter the keywords "atlas of dinosaurs".

Help

For general help and advice on using the Internet, go to the Usborne Quicklinks Website and click on "Net Help".

To find out more about using your web browser, click on your browser's Help menu and choose "Contents and Index". You'll find a searchable dictionary containing tips on how to find your way around the Internet easily.

What you need

The websites described in this book can be accessed using a standard home computer and a web browser (the software that enables you to display information from the Internet). Here's a list of the basic requirements:

- A PC with Microsoft® Windows® 98 or a later version, or a Macintosh computer with System 9.0 or later

- 64Mb RAM

- A web browser such as Microsoft® Internet Explorer 5, or Netscape® Navigator 4.7, or later versions

- Connection to the Internet via a modem (preferably 56kbps) or a faster digital or cable line

- An account with an Internet Service Provider (ISP)

- A sound card to hear sound files

Computer viruses

A computer virus is a program that can damage your computer. A virus can get into your computer when you download programs from the Internet, or in an attachment (an extra file) that arrives with an email. We strongly recommend that you buy anti-virus software to protect your computer and that you update the software regularly. You can buy anti-virus software at computer stores or download it from the Internet. To find out more about viruses, go to Usborne Quicklinks and click on "Net Help".

Extras

Some websites need additional programs, called plug-ins, to play sounds, or to show videos, animations or 3-D images. If you go to a site and you do not have the necessary plug-in, a message should come up on the screen.

There is usually a button on the site that you can click on to download the plug-in. Alternatively, go to Usborne Quicklinks and click on "Net Help". There you can find links to download plug-ins. Here is a list of plug-ins that you might need:

- QuickTime – lets you play video clips.

- RealOne Player® – lets you play video clips and sound files.

- Flash™ – lets you play animations.

- Shockwave® – lets you play animations and enjoy interactive sites.

★

Downloadable pictures

Pictures in this book marked with a ★ symbol can be downloaded from the Usborne Quicklinks Website for your own personal use. The pictures are the copyright of Usborne Publishing and may not be used for any commercial or profit-related purpose. To download a picture, go to the Usborne Quicklinks Website and follow the instructions there.

Saying dinosaur names

For a pronunciation guide to dinosaur names, and the names of other prehistoric animals, go to the Usborne Quicklinks Website and follow the instructions there.

Internet safety

- Ask your parent's or guardian's permission before you connect to the Internet. They can then stay nearby if they think they should do so. If you are using someone else's computer, always check first that it is all right for you to connect to the Internet.

- If you write a message in a website guest book or on a website message board, do not include your email address, real name, address or telephone number.

- If a website asks you to log in or register by typing your name or email address, ask the permission of an adult first.

- If you receive email from someone you don't know, tell an adult and do not reply to the email.

- Never arrange to meet anyone you have talked to on the Internet.

Note for parents

The websites described in this book are regularly checked and reviewed by Usborne editors and the links in Usborne Quicklinks are updated. However, the content of a website may change at any time and Usborne Publishing is not responsible for the content of any website other than its own.

We recommend that children are supervised while on the Internet, that they do not use Internet chat rooms, and that you use Internet filtering software to block unsuitable material.

Please ensure that your children read and follow the safety guidelines above. For more information, go to the Net Help area on the Usborne Quicklinks Website at **www.usborne-quicklinks.com**

Incredible animals

Around 240 million years ago, long before people existed, a new group of animals appeared on Earth. They were the dinosaurs. They included some of the largest ever land animals and some of the deadliest predators. No one has ever seen a live dinosaur, as they all died out 65 million years ago.

Reptiles with a difference

Dinosaurs were reptiles. Like other reptiles, such as crocodiles and lizards, dinosaurs laid eggs and had scaly, waterproof skin. Most reptiles have legs that stick out sideways from their bodies, but dinosaurs' legs supported their bodies from underneath. This meant dinosaurs' legs were stronger than other reptiles'.

Dinosaur variety

There were many different kinds, or species, of dinosaurs. Some were no bigger than a hen, while others grew to more than ten times the size of an elephant. Meat-eating dinosaurs had razor-sharp teeth whereas some plant-eating dinosaurs had toothless beaks. There were dinosaurs with horns on their faces, crests on their heads and some even had frills around their necks.

PRECAMBRIAN PERIOD

The first soft-bodied creatures

550 MYA

CAMBRIAN PERIOD
The first creatures with skeletons

510 MYA

The first fish

The first land plants

ORDOVICIAN PERIOD

440 MYA

The first creatures on land

SILURIAN PERIOD

408 MYA

The first amphibians

DEVONIAN PERIOD

362 MYA

The first flying insects

Tsintaosaurus had a bony head crest.

Carnotaurus had stout horns on its head.

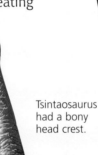

Gallimimus had a toothless beak.

When did they live?

Dinosaurs lived in a time known as the Mesozoic era, which lasted from 250 to 65 million years ago. The Mesozoic era is divided into three periods: the Triassic (when the first dinosaurs appeared), the Jurassic and the Cretaceous. Each dinosaur species lived for a few million years and new species developed all the time. Dinosaurs dominated the Earth for 175 million years and were one of the most successful animal groups of all time.

🦕 **Internet link**

For a link to a website where you can watch a short movie about dinosaurs and test your knowledge with a quiz, go to www.usborne-quicklinks.com

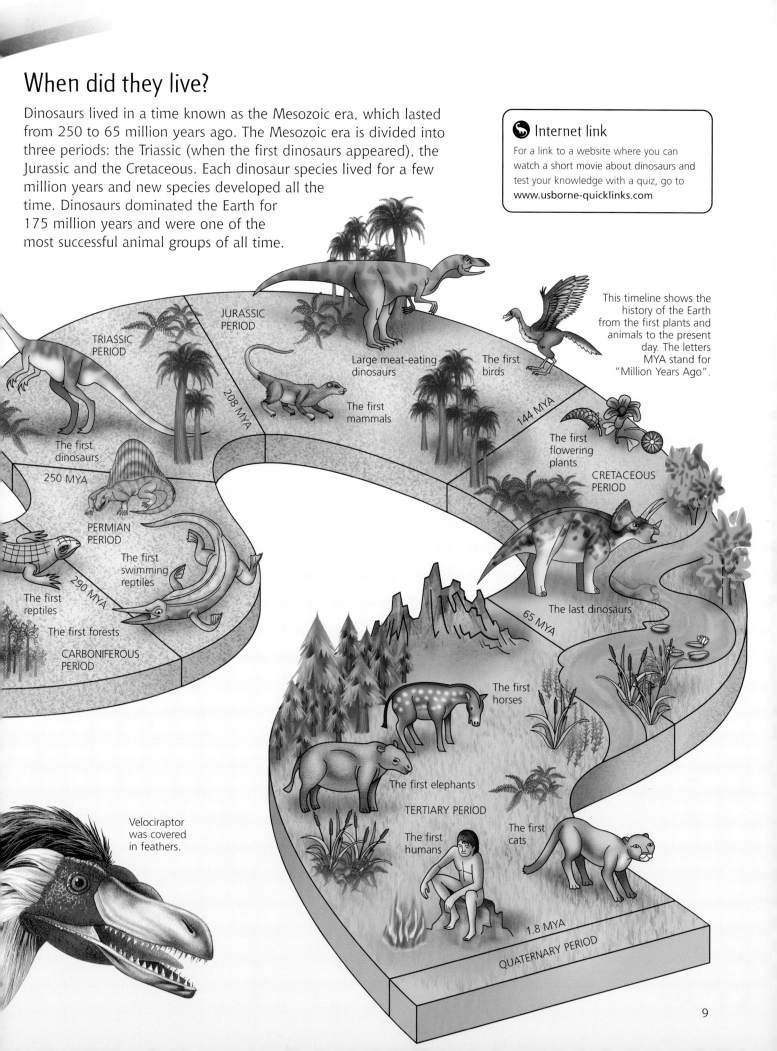

This timeline shows the history of the Earth from the first plants and animals to the present day. The letters MYA stand for "Million Years Ago".

JURASSIC PERIOD

TRIASSIC PERIOD

Large meat-eating dinosaurs

The first birds

208 MYA

The first mammals

The first dinosaurs

250 MYA

144 MYA

The first flowering plants

CRETACEOUS PERIOD

PERMIAN PERIOD

The first swimming reptiles

290 MYA

The first reptiles

The first forests

CARBONIFEROUS PERIOD

The last dinosaurs

65 MYA

Velociraptor was covered in feathers.

The first horses

The first elephants

TERTIARY PERIOD

The first humans

The first cats

1.8 MYA

QUATERNARY PERIOD

9

Dividing up dinosaurs

So far, more than 900 different kinds of dinosaurs have been discovered. To work out how all the different dinosaurs are related to each other, scientists divide them into groups, according to the features they shared.

Lizard and bird hips

Dinosaurs are divided into two main groups: saurischian dinosaurs and ornithischian dinosaurs. Saurischians had hipbones that were similar in shape to modern lizards' hipbones. Ornithischians had hipbones similar to modern birds' hipbones.

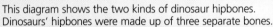

This diagram shows the two kinds of dinosaur hipbones. Dinosaurs' hipbones were made up of three separate bones.

Ornithischian dinosaurs had pubis bones (shown in pink) that pointed back.

Saurischian dinosaurs had pubis bones that pointed forward.

The biggest group

Ornithischians made up the largest group of dinosaurs. They were all herbivores and many of them lived in herds. Ornithischians are divided into five main groups: stegosaurs, pachycephalosaurs, ornithopods, ceratopsians and ankylosaurs.

Ornithopods were the most common type of ornithischian. They ranged from the smallest of the hypsilophodontids, which were only around 1m (3ft) long, to the larger iguanodontids and hadrosaurs, which grew up to 15m (49ft) long.

⬡ **Internet link**

For a link to a website where you can find out more about different kinds of dinosaurs and how scientists divide them up, go to www.usborne-quicklinks.com

Stegosaurus   Pachycephalosaurus   Triceratops   Ankylosaurus

Hypsilophodon

Stegosaurs had bony plates on their bodies. The plates were not very strong and may have been used for display.	Pachycephalosaurs had thick, domed skulls. They were fast-moving and walked on two legs.	Hypsilophodon was an ornithopod dinosaur. Ornithopods had strong teeth for chewing vegetation. They walked on two or four legs and foraged for food on all fours.	Like most ceratopsians, Triceratops had bony frills at the back of its skull and sharp horns on its face for scaring off enemies.	Ankylosaurs were the best-protected ornithischians. Their bodies were covered in thick, bony spikes and plates.

Like many theropods, Tyrannosaurus had sharp, serrated teeth for ripping chunks of meat off other animals.

Theropods' sharp claws helped them to catch their prey.

Plant-eaters and predators

Saurischian dinosaurs are divided into sauropodomorphs and theropods. Most sauropodomorphs were herbivores. They walked on four legs most of the time and had long necks and tails. Sauropodomorphs included the largest and heaviest dinosaurs.

Theropods were the killers of the dinosaur world. They were fast-moving animals that walked on two legs. Most of them were carnivores and many had sharp teeth and claws that were well-suited to catching and eating prey.

Tyrannosaurus walked on two powerful back legs.

Theropods had four toes but only walked on three. The first toe was held just above the ground.

Dinosaur relations

This chart shows how some of the different groups of dinosaurs are related to each other. The dinosaur shown at the end of each branch is one example of the many different species each group contains.

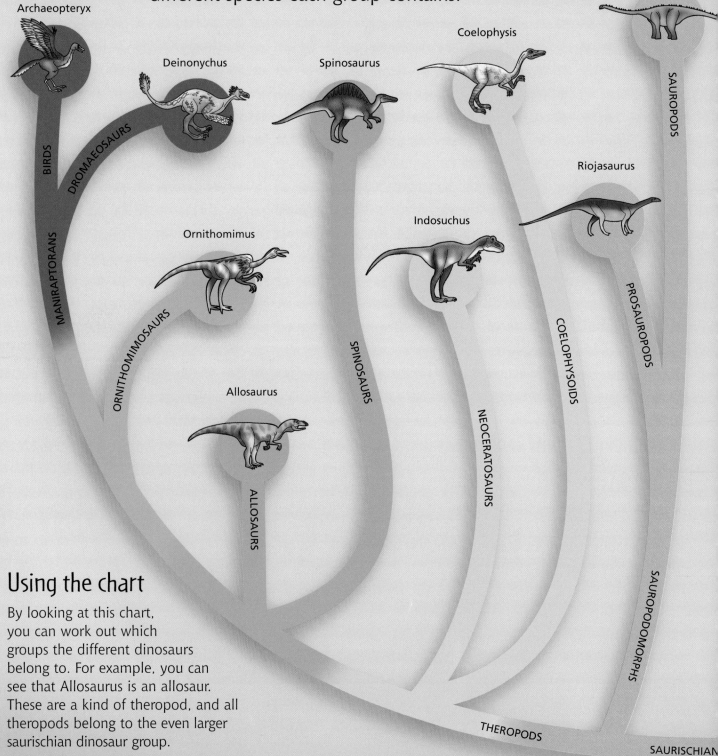

Archaeopteryx

Deinonychus

Spinosaurus

Coelophysis

Diplodocus

Ornithomimus

Indosuchus

Riojasaurus

Allosaurus

BIRDS

DROMAEOSAURS

MANIRAPTORANS

ORNITHOMIMOSAURS

ALLOSAURS

SPINOSAURS

NEOCERATOSAURS

COELOPHYSOIDS

PROSAUROPODS

SAUROPODS

SAUROPODOMORPHS

THEROPODS

SAURISCHIAN

Using the chart

By looking at this chart, you can work out which groups the different dinosaurs belong to. For example, you can see that Allosaurus is an allosaur. These are a kind of theropod, and all theropods belong to the even larger saurischian dinosaur group.

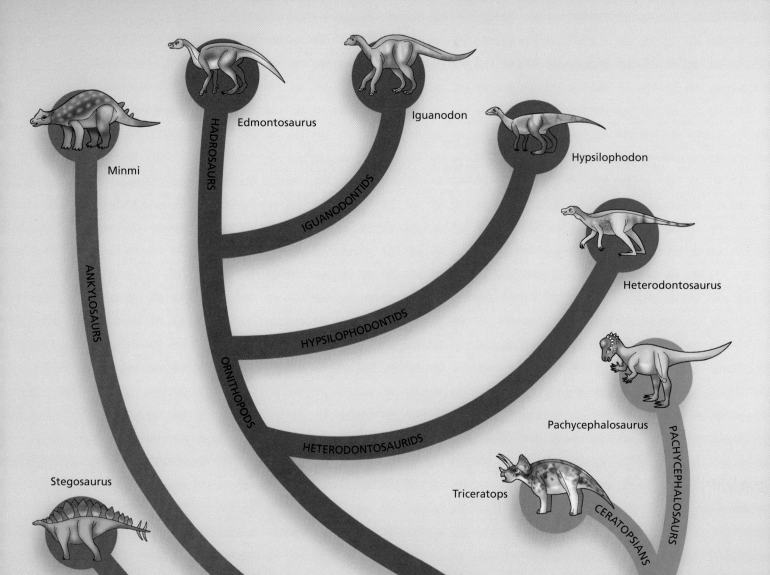

Minmi

Edmontosaurus

Iguanodon

Hypsilophodon

Heterodontosaurus

Pachycephalosaurus

Triceratops

Stegosaurus

Lesothosaurus

ANKYLOSAURS

HADROSAURS

IGUANODONTIDS

HYPSILOPHODONTIDS

ORNITHOPODS

HETERODONTOSAURIDS

STEGOSAURS

THYREOPHORANS

LESOTHOSAURS

CERATOPSIANS

PACHYCEPHALOSAURS

MARGINOCEPHALIANS

DINOSAURS

ORNITHISCHIANS

Shared features

Each group is made up
of dinosaurs that shared
certain features. Thyreophorans,
for example, all had bony plates along
their backs. Sometimes, members of a group
may look very different, but have similar
structures in common. For example,
maniraptorans all share similar wrist joints.

Fantastic fossils

Some dinosaurs were preserved in rocks after they died. By studying their remains, known as fossils, scientists can find out an enormous amount about them, even though they died out millions of years ago.

🦕 Internet link

For a link to a website where you can find out more about different kinds of fossils and see how dinosaurs became fossils, go to www.usborne-quicklinks.com

Buried bones

It is very rare for dead animals to become fossils. Usually, they are eaten and their bones are scattered by other animals, or they just rot away. However, as there were millions of dinosaurs, there are a lot of dinosaur fossils. Most fossils form when an animal dies in or near water, and is quickly buried by particles of mud and sand, known as sediment.

Stegosaurus had plates along its neck, back and tail. The plates made Stegosaurus look more intimidating and may have helped it to attract mates.

This is a fossilized skeleton of a Stegosaurus. The fossil is almost complete, so scientists have a good idea of what Stegosaurus was like.

Stegosaurus had a straight neck when it was alive. The fossil has a bent neck because after death the muscles in the neck contracted, giving the neck a curved shape. The small pieces of bone beneath the neck formed a protective throat pouch.

The three bones to the right make up the dinosaur's hipbones, or pelvis.

The short feet and wide legs suggest this was a slow-moving animal.

The five strong, wide toe bones on the front feet would have helped to support its weight.

14

Becoming a fossil

Over millions of years, sediment builds up in layers over an animal's body. Each layer presses down on the one below, making the sediment slowly turn into rock. Rock formed like this is known as sedimentary rock. Chemicals in the rock then seep into tiny holes in the bones and teeth of the animal. The chemicals very gradually become hard and the animal skeleton becomes a fossil. The fossilized hard parts of an animal, such as its teeth and bones, are called body fossils.

★

A dinosaur dies near water. Its flesh soon begins to rot away, leaving only the bones behind.

Water levels rise and cover the bones. Sediment builds up over them, stopping them from being swept away.

The sediment gradually turns into rock, trapping the animal's body between its layers.

Trace fossils

Scientists have also found fossilized footprints, leaves with bite marks in them, and even dinosaur dung. These are called trace fossils, as they reveal traces of how dinosaurs lived. Trace fossils form differently from body fossils. Fossil footprints, for example, can form when an animal treads in soft mud, which hardens into rock over time, preserving the shape of the footprint.

Mummified dinosaurs

Very few dinosaurs have been found with their flesh and muscles preserved. This only happened when a dinosaur's body dried out very quickly, in hot, dry conditions, so that the flesh didn't rot. This process is known as mummification.

What fossils tell us

People who study fossils are called paleontologists. Paleontologists use body fossils to find out about dinosaurs' shapes and sizes. Fossil footprints give clues about how they lived. Lots of similar footprints found together, for example, suggest that some dinosaurs lived in herds.

The plates decreased in size along the tail. No two plates have exactly the same size or shape.

The back legs are longer than the front legs. This would have made Stegosaurus' head tilt down, close to the ground.

These are tail spikes, which Stegosaurus used to defend itself.

This is a piece of fossilized dinosaur dung. Fossils of dinosaur dung are rarer than body fossils, as dung decays quickly.

Fossilized dung, called coprolites, can show what dinosaurs ate. Coprolites from herbivores contain plant material, while coprolites from carnivores contain splinters of bone.

Hunting for fossils

Sometimes people stumble across dinosaur fossils by chance, but most fossils are found by paleontologists on organized expeditions. These expeditions often last for many years and can take place in difficult and dangerous conditions.

 Internet link

For a link to a website where you can read about some amazing fossil sites around the world, go to www.usborne-quicklinks.com

This is Dinosaur Provincial Park in Alberta, Canada. Its vast areas of exposed Mesozoic rock make it a perfect place to look for dinosaurs.

Where to look

Fossils are found only in sedimentary rock, so paleontologists look for dinosaur fossils in sedimentary rock that was formed when the dinosaurs were alive, during the Mesozoic era. Even though dinosaurs only lived on land, their bodies were often carried out to sea by rivers or floods, so paleontologists also look in areas that were seas or oceans during the Mesozoic era.

Hunting grounds

Much of the sedimentary rock from the Mesozoic era is buried deep underground. To find dinosaur fossils, paleontologists look at areas where the rocks above have been worn away by rivers or the sea, exposing the Mesozoic rock. Mesozoic rock is also exposed where people have mined into rocks or where they have cut through rocks to build roads.

This fossil of dinosaur Conchoraptor is from the Gobi Desert. The strong winds that blow through the Gobi Desert have eroded the layers of rock above, revealing fossils at the surface.

Top spots

The best sites for dinosaur fossils are where large areas of rock are continually being eroded. These areas are usually remote deserts or bare, rocky land known as badlands. Badlands have steep, narrow valleys and little or no vegetation, which makes it easy to see any fossils sticking out of the rock.

These hadrosaur bones are sticking out of sedimentary rock in badlands in North America.

Hidden fossils

Unfortunately, scientists are unable to explore all the sedimentary rock from the Mesozoic era. Some Mesozoic rock is too deeply buried under other rocks, soil, water or even buildings. There are many dinosaur fossils that will never be found. Fossils in cliffs, for example, are often washed away before people can get to them. Areas can also be difficult to reach because of wars, political problems or harsh weather conditions.

Chance discoveries

Some amazing chance discoveries have been made by farmers and people working on roads and rail tracks. One of the most exciting recent finds was made by a farmer in Patagonia, Argentina. He stumbled across some stumps sticking out of the ground, which scientists later discovered were the neck bones of one of the longest dinosaurs. This dinosaur has not yet been named.

Digging for dinosaurs

The process of excavating, transporting and cleaning dinosaur fossils is difficult and time-consuming. It can take scientists months, or even years, to prepare and examine dinosaur bones. Until this is done, the significance of a find is not known.

Internet link

For a link to a website where you can find out useful information on how dinosaur bones are excavated, go to www.usborne-quicklinks.com

Uncovering fossils

When a fossil has been discovered, experts carefully clear away the rock and soil around it using picks, shovels, hammers and brushes. Sections of hard rock can be removed using power tools or even explosives. A wide area around the fossil is also studied closely, as more bones from the same dinosaur may be buried nearby.

This photograph shows a team of American paleontologists excavating dinosaur bones in Africa. They use hammers, chisels and other tools to clear away rock and sand.

Keeping a record

Once experts have uncovered all the fossils at a site, they measure, photograph, draw and label each one. The exact position of every fragment is meticulously recorded. These details will be essential when reconstructing the skeleton.

Paleontologists work methodically and neatly, clearing away rock debris as they go, so it doesn't become mixed up with fossil fragments.

Moving fossils

When fossils are removed from the site, they are wrapped to prevent damage. Small fossils can be covered in paper and put in bags, while larger bones are encased in plaster. Often, fossils are still partly embedded in rock, so the rock is covered in plaster too. Some fossils are so heavy that they have to be moved using a crane.

★

Strips of material are soaked in plaster and put onto large fossils. The plaster sets quickly, becoming a hard shell.

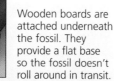
Wooden boards are attached underneath the fossil. They provide a flat base so the fossil doesn't roll around in transit.

A paleontologist uses fine tools to scrape rock from Tyrannosaurus bones. Behind him are more bones in plaster, waiting to be cleaned.

Careful cleaning

The cleaning and preparation of fossils takes place in a laboratory. First, the protective layers are cut away, and then any rock around the bones is sandblasted off or dissolved in weak acid solutions. Next, scientists slowly pick away the last traces of rock with a needle or dental drill, using a magnifying glass or microscope to see fine details. The bones are strengthened with chemical solutions so they don't crumble, and are stored in a safe place.

This fossil site is in the Sahara Desert, where paleontologists work for hours in extremely hot, dry conditions.

Looking inside

Some fossils, such as skulls and unhatched eggs, are filled with rock. It is impossible to remove this rock without cutting into the fossil. However, sophisticated x-ray scanners have now been developed that highlight the shape of fossils within rock. Using these scanners, scientists can find out information such as the size of a brain cavity within a skull, or the position of a baby inside an egg.

This is an illustration of an x-ray, showing a dinosaur inside an egg.

Identifying dinosaurs

Paleontologists sometimes have very little to work on when they attempt to identify a newly discovered dinosaur skeleton. They carefully examine all the bones they find to look for clues to the dinosaur's identity. But if many bones are missing or bones are jumbled up with the bones of other animals, mistakes can sometimes be made.

Skull shapes

Many types of dinosaurs had skulls with distinctive shapes. This means that paleontologists can usually identify a dinosaur from its skull, as long as enough of the skull is found. For example, stegosaurs had very long, tapered skulls, most pachycephalosaurs had very thick, dome-shaped skulls and ceratopsians usually had frills on the backs of their skulls.

Stegosaurus' narrow, long skull had a toothless beak at the end of the snout.

Diagnostic bones

If the skull or part of the skull is missing, identifying a dinosaur can be more difficult. Paleontologists have to look for parts of the skeleton that are unique to a particular type of dinosaur. These parts are known as the diagnostic bones. Pachycephalosaurs, for example, all had very long ribs connecting their backbones to their pelvic bones. No other dinosaurs had ribs like these.

Internet link

For a link to a website where you can find out more about the tooth shapes of different types of dinosaurs, go to www.usborne-quicklinks.com

Telling teeth

Teeth can also help to identify dinosaurs, as different types of dinosaurs had very different teeth. For example, sauropods had either spoon-shaped or peg-like teeth, and theropods had very sharp, pointed teeth.

Dinosaur teeth were adapted to help them to eat specific types of food. So, even if it's not possible to say exactly which type of dinosaur a tooth belonged to, it's still possible to say what sort of diet it had.

Brachiosaurus ripped tough leaves off plants with its chisel-shaped teeth.

Stegosaurus had small teeth with ridges, for slicing through vegetation.

Allosaurus had sharp teeth with serrated edges, which helped it to eat meat.

This is the skeleton of Archaeoraptor with ultraviolet light shining on it. The ultraviolet light makes it easier to see the different bones.

Feathery fake

Sometimes, "new" dinosaurs turn out to be fakes. In 1999, a fossil that appeared to be the remains of a bird-like dinosaur was found. It was given the name Archaeoraptor. It had wings like a bird's and a reptile's tail.

However, on much closer examination, paleontologists discovered many tiny breaks in Archaeoraptor's skeleton, some of which had been skillfully plastered over to try to conceal them. The paleontologists realized that someone had stuck together fossilized dinosaur and bird bones to make what looked like a complete skeleton.

Mistaken identity

Paleontologists occasionally think they have identified a new species of dinosaur when what they have actually found are the bones of different dinosaurs jumbled together.

For example, in 1906, a tyrannosaur was discovered that seemed to have protective plates on it. It was declared a new species and was given the name Dynamosaurus imperiosus. Later, paleontologists discovered that the plates belonged to an ankylosaur, and that the tyrannosaur was a Tyrannosaurus rex.

The body of Archaeoraptor belonged to a bird.

This is the tail bone. It belonged to dinosaur Microraptor.

Bringing bones to life

Reconstructing dinosaurs is an essential part of a paleontologist's job. The first step is to rebuild the skeleton. But by using fossil evidence and making comparisons with modern animals, scientists can go much further than this.

🦕 Internet link

For a link to a website where you can read about the first ever dinosaur skeleton to be put on display, go to www.usborne-quicklinks.com

Building up bones

Putting a dinosaur skeleton back together requires a lot of detective work. Paleontologists frequently have as little as 20% of a skeleton to work with, and sometimes much less. So the first thing they need to do is find out what the missing bones looked like.

If bones belonging to the same species of dinosaur have already been discovered, scientists can work out which bones are missing from each skeleton by comparing the sets of bones. They can then make replicas of the missing ones.

These paleontologists are preparing a Baryonyx skeleton for display in a museum. Before they connect the bones together, they lay them out on the floor in their correct positions.

This is a reconstruction of Baryonyx in the position its fossil was found in. Paleontologists have added muscles and skin to its basic skeleton.

Building muscles

If a complete dinosaur skeleton is built up, then muscles can be added onto it. This provides a much clearer idea of what the living dinosaur would have looked like. The muscles of animals alive today are often used as guides to how dinosaurs' muscles were arranged. Sometimes, the marks where muscles were attached to bones are preserved. These enable paleontologists to tell how big and what shape the muscles were.

Changing views

Theories about dinosaurs are constantly changing as new evidence comes to light. For example, people used to think that dinosaurs' nostrils were high up on their snouts. New research indicates that many types of dinosaurs had nostrils very close to the tips of their snouts. This discovery could help scientists to find out more about how dinosaurs breathed and smelled.

Skin and feathers

Very rarely, fossilized dinosaur skin and fossilized imprints of dinosaur skin are discovered. These can show what the texture of the dinosaur's skin was like, and whether or not it had any feathers. However, they don't show what shade the skin was, so scientists have to use their imaginations when reconstructing this.

Until recently, scientists thought that Tyrannosaurus' nostrils were high up on its snout.

Tyrannosaurus' nostrils are now thought to have been at the end of its snout, much closer to the mouth, as shown here.

Back from the dead

In the movie Jurassic Park, scientists bring dinosaurs back to life. They do this by using a substance called DNA, which was once part of a dinosaur, to make copies of the original dinosaur. But is this really possible?

Internet link

For a link to a website where you can find out more about recreating dinosaurs, go to www.usborne-quicklinks.com

These velociraptors are recreated using ancient dinosaur DNA, in the movie *Jurassic Park*.

Design for life

DNA is a very complex chemical found in every living thing. It is like a design or plan. What you look like, how tall you are likely to grow and even some aspects of your personality depend on how the different components of your DNA are arranged. It also contains all the information that scientists need to recreate an animal.

This is Dolly the sheep. She was the first mammal to be made from an adult animal's DNA.

How it works

So far, scientists have successfully recreated several different types of animals, including sheep, cats, mice and pigs. This procedure is known as cloning. They do it by taking some of an animal's DNA and putting it in an egg cell. They then place the egg in a suitable mother animal, where it grows into a baby animal. The new animal, which is known as a clone, is an exact copy of the original.

Ancient DNA

The main problem scientists face if they want to clone a dinosaur is where to find dinosaur DNA. No dinosaur fossil found so far has contained any DNA. But, scientists have found prehistoric blood-sucking insects preserved inside fossilized tree resin. If one of these insects fed on dinosaur blood, some of that blood may have been preserved, and in it some dinosaur DNA.

DNA decay

So far, no one has found any dinosaur DNA in insect blood. Even if some were found, many scientists think that it still wouldn't be possible to use it to clone a dinosaur. Successful cloning requires near-perfect DNA. But DNA begins to decay after about ten thousand years. Even the most recent dinosaur DNA would be much older than this and would have broken down too much to be of any use.

This insect was trapped in tree resin millions of years ago. The resin then hardened, preserving the insect inside it.

Jungle dinosaurs

Scientists may not be able to bring dinosaurs back to life, but could any dinosaurs have survived and still be alive today? People living in the jungle of the Congo, in Africa, claim to have seen a sauropod-like animal which they call mokele mbembe. They say it's about the size of a small elephant, and lives in swamps, feeding off plants.

It's not impossible that a large, unknown animal could live undetected in the depths of the jungle. But scientists investigating the case think that mokele mbembe may actually be a rhinoceros, and not a dinosaur.

This is a dingiso tree kangaroo. Until 1994, no one knew these animals existed. If they could remain undiscovered for so long, perhaps there are larger animals, such as dinosaurs, waiting to be discovered as well.

Plant-eating dinosaurs roamed in herds for protection against meat-eaters.

Dinosaur world

Here you can find out what the world was like in the age of the dinosaurs. You can also discover how dinosaurs developed over time, how they are related to birds and study the mystery behind the extinction of the dinosaurs.

Changing Earth

The Earth looked very different when dinosaurs were alive. Since then, new oceans have formed, continents have changed position and new mountains have appeared. This is all due to the movement of huge pieces of rock, called plates, which make up the Earth's surface.

Shifting continents

The Earth is made up of different layers. The plates that make up the Earth's surface, or crust, lie on top of a layer called the mantle. Parts of the mantle are molten (melted). These parts are constantly moving, and as they move, they drag the plates with them. The plates only move at a rate of about 5cm (2in) a year. But over millions of years this is enough to make the continents shift huge distances. When dinosaurs first appeared, the continents were in very different positions from where they are now.

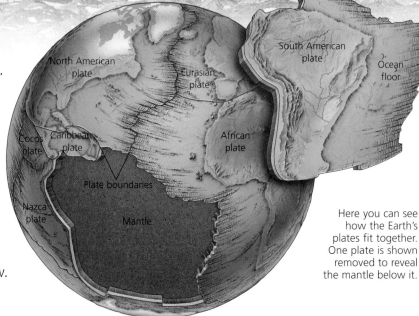

North American plate

Eurasian plate

South American plate

Ocean floor

Cocos plate

Caribbean plate

African plate

Plate boundaries

Nazca plate

Mantle

Here you can see how the Earth's plates fit together. One plate is shown removed to reveal the mantle below it.

Moving mountains

When dinosaurs lived, some mountain ranges had not yet formed. The Himalayas, for example, formed five million years after dinosaurs died out, when the two huge plates that make up India and Asia collided with each other. The crust buckled up to form the world's highest mountain range. Mountains that form like this, when two plates collide, are known as fold mountains.

These mountains are part of the Himalayas. The Himalayas run along the border of present-day India and China.

Ocean changes

The movement of the plates also changes the size and shape of the oceans. When two plates collide with each other on the ocean floor, one of the plates is pushed under the other, where it melts back into the mantle. In other places, plates drift away from each other. Magma rises up to fill the gap, widening the ocean.

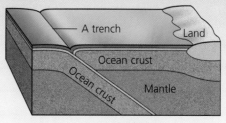

A trench
Land
Ocean crust
Ocean crust
Mantle

This diagram shows what happens when two plates on the ocean floor collide. A deep crack, known as a trench, forms between the two plates.

Fossil evidence

Fossils help us to find out how the continents have moved around. Paleontologists often find fossils of the same types of animals on continents that are now separated from each other by massive oceans. In order for the animals to have spread between them, the continents must have been joined together when those animals were alive.

This is a fossil of the dinosaur Hypsilophodon. Fossils like this one have been found in both North America and Europe, suggesting that Europe was once joined to North America.

Maps of the Mesozoic era

These maps show the positions of the oceans and continents during the Mesozoic era. The maps range from the Triassic period to the end of the Cretaceous period, when the continents were beginning to move closer to where they are today.

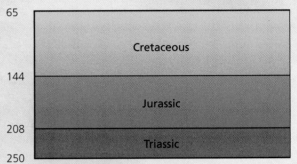

This chart shows the timescale of the Mesozoic era. The figures on the left show how many millions of years ago each period was.

The supercontinent

At the beginning of the Triassic period, most of the continents were joined together as one giant supercontinent, called Pangaea. Surrounding Pangaea was the huge Panthalassa Ocean, which covered two-thirds of Earth's surface. Only China and part of southeast Asia were separate from Pangaea.

This map shows Pangaea at the beginning of the Triassic period. The white lines encircle the land that makes up today's continents. Sometimes, parts of the modern continents were covered with water, which is why some white lines are in the sea.

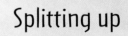

Splitting up

Most of the continents remained joined together as Pangaea at the end of the Triassic period. However, some parts of Africa, North America and Europe had begun to drift away from each other. The rifting between north Africa and the eastern coast of North America led to the formation of the North Atlantic Ocean.

In some places, the crust between North America and Europe collapsed, to form a series of deep, wide valleys, known as rift valleys.

Drifting apart

During the Jurassic period, Pangaea split in two, to form Laurasia in the north and Gondwana in the south. Sea levels rose, and shallow seas flooded parts of the continents. The North Atlantic Ocean continued to widen and North America and Africa drifted farther away from each other.

For much of the Jurassic period, Europe was divided into a series of islands.

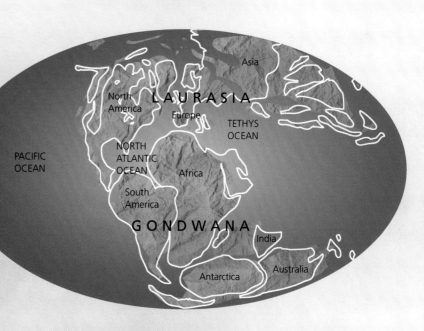

Separate continents

In the early Cretaceous period, shallow seas continued to divide the continents into separate islands. The continents also continued to drift apart. Antarctica and Australia moved farther from Africa and South America, and the Atlantic Ocean continued to widen.

India continued to move farther away from Africa, Antarctica and Australia.

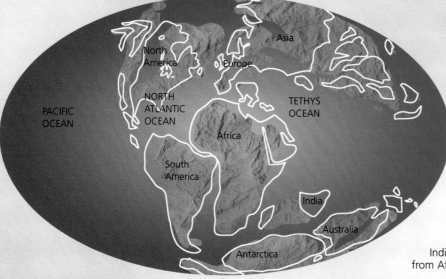

Rising seas

At the end of the Cretaceous period, sea levels were much higher than they are today. An inland sea divided North America into eastern and western halves, and much of Europe was underwater. There was also a big inland sea dividing north Africa. Most of the major continents were separated by oceans.

During the Cretaceous period there was an occasional land link between North America and Asia.

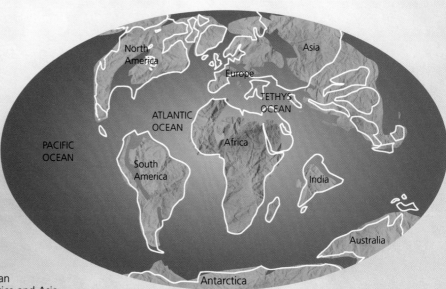

Triassic world

In the Triassic period, the animals and plants were very different from those around today. Reptiles dominated the land and skies, and there were no grasses or flowering plants. It was during this time that dinosaurs first appeared.

Flying reptiles, called pterosaurs, first appeared in the Triassic period.

Hot and dry

The Earth is hottest near the Equator, where the Sun's rays hit its surface full on. When the dinosaurs first appeared, Pangaea lay across the Equator. This meant most of Pangaea was receiving direct rays from the Sun, making the land hotter than it is today. Vast deserts stretched across the middle of Pangaea and there was no ice on the poles.

Living by the sea

Places near the sea have a milder and wetter climate than areas inland. Pangaea's huge size meant that large areas of land were very far from the coast. These inland areas received very little rain. Fossils from the Triassic period show that dinosaurs lived mostly near the coast, in the wetter areas and scrublands of Pangaea, although some may have lived in the deserts.

This is a typical late Triassic scene, with animals gathering around the edge of a lake.

Postosuchus was a large, crocodile-like archosaur. It probably hunted alone.

Coelophysis were small predatory dinosaurs. They lived in groups for protection against larger predators.

Horsetail plants grew mostly in damp areas.

32

Triassic reptiles

During the Triassic period, there were three main types of reptiles on land: dinosaurs, crocodile-like archosaurs and pterosaurs. The crocodile-like archosaurs were large, heavy animals that walked on four legs. In the late Triassic period, they were the most common land animals. Dinosaurs made up only around 5% of all land animals.

A time of change

The very first dinosaurs were small and were hunted by crocodile-like archosaurs, which were many times their size. But, by the end of the Triassic period dinosaurs had started to increase in size, while the crocodile-like archosaurs were dying out. The age of the dinosaurs had begun.

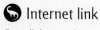

Internet link

For a link to an interactive website where you can find out more about Triassic plants and animals, go to www.usborne-quicklinks.com

Cycad trees were very common in the Triassic period.

Plateosaurs were plant-eating dinosaurs. They grew up to 7m (23ft) long.

Plateosaurs could rear up on their back legs to feed. They used their tails for extra support.

Jurassic world

During the Jurassic period, dinosaurs spread all over the Earth. The first birds appeared too, although the skies were still dominated by flying reptiles. The rivers were filled with crocodiles and large reptiles called plesiosaurs, while dolphin-like ichthyosaurs, sharks and plesiosaurs swam in the seas and oceans.

This shows a scene from mid-Jurassic China. A diverse array of dinosaurs lived there, including stegosaurs, sauropods and theropods.

Plesiosaurs lived in water, but had to come to the surface to breathe.

Hsisosuchus was a Jurassic crocodile. It had longer legs than crocodiles today and spent more time on land.

Warm and wet

As Pangaea broke up during the Jurassic period, huge seas formed between the continents. Sea levels rose, and large sections of the continents were flooded. The world was cooler and more humid than it had been during the Triassic period, but it was still warmer than it is today. In this mild, wet climate, areas that had been desert during the Triassic period became covered in lush vegetation, and huge forests grew over large parts of the Earth.

Plesiosaurs had four paddle-shaped flippers, which they used to push themselves through the water.

Huayangosaurs were stegosaurs. They had sharp spikes on their tails, which helped to protect them against attack.

Dinosaur giants

New and extraordinary types
of plant-eating dinosaurs
flourished during the
Jurassic period. Stegosaurs
and ankylosaurs, for
example, had protective plates
and spikes on their bodies. Perhaps
the most amazing dinosaurs were the
long-necked sauropods, which were
the largest land animals of all time.

Shunosaurs were
medium-sized sauropods that
lived together in herds. Unlike
other sauropods, they had
clubs on the end of their tails.

Jurassic killers

Many of the theropod dinosaurs from the
Jurassic period were huge. Some grew up
to 12m (39ft) long and were capable of
killing even the largest sauropods.
Smaller theropods were probably just
as common, but fewer of them
became fossils, because their
light, hollow bones were
easily crushed
and scattered.

Gasosaurus was
a theropod. It
had sharp teeth,
which it used
to tear flesh
from its prey.

Huayangosaurs grew
to around 4m (13ft)
long. They fed on
plants growing close
to the ground, such
as ferns and
baby cycads.

35

Cretaceous world

Dinosaurs lived all over the world during the Cretaceous period. Many new species of dinosaurs developed, and many of the animals and plants around today appeared for the first time. These included new groups of mammals and insects, as well as many different kinds of birds.

By the Cretaceous period, birds had diversified and spread to many parts of the world. Rahonavis was a primitive bird with slashing claws on its second toes.

This is a late Cretaceous scene from northwest Madagascar, showing some of the different dinosaurs that were common in the southern continents at the time.

Abelisaur Majungatholus was a huge theropod dinosaur. It preyed on sauropods and other large plant-eaters.

The first flowers

The biggest change between the Jurassic and Cretaceous period was the appearance of flowering plants. By the middle of the Cretaceous period, they had begun to spread across the world and had developed into many different species. Bees, wasps and butterflies, which fed on the flowering plants, also appeared for the first time.

The first flowering plants were probably bright to help attract insects.

Dragonflies were among the first flying insects, first appearing over 300 million years ago. They were common during the Cretaceous period.

Different dinosaurs

There were more dinosaur species in the late Cretaceous period than at any other time. New types of ornithopod dinosaurs were appearing, especially in North America, while elsewhere the large sauropods remained some of the most abundant plant-eaters. There was a greater diversity of theropod dinosaurs, including the horned abelisaurs in the southern continents, and the giant tyrannosaurs in the north.

🐾 Internet link

For a link to a website where you can find out more about the different plants and animals of the Cretaceous period, go to www.usborne-quicklinks.com

Masiakasaurus was a small theropod dinosaur, only growing to 2m (7ft) long. Scientists think it may have fed on fish.

Changing climate

The Cretaceous climate was warm, with wet and dry seasons. Tropical seas stretched as far north as London and New York, and temperatures never fell below freezing. Then at the very end of the Cretaceous period there were some dramatic climate changes. Sea levels dropped, temperatures changed and in some parts of the world there were lots of volcanic eruptions. These changes could be part of the reason why dinosaurs became extinct.

Rapetosaurus belonged to a group of sauropods called titanosaurs. Titanosaurs were different from other sauropods as they had bony lumps of skin on their bodies.

Masiakasaurus had strange, forward-pointing teeth, which it may have used to help it catch fish.

Evolution

Most scientists believe that living things gradually change over time. This idea is called the theory of evolution. Scientists use the theory of evolution to try to work out where dinosaurs came from and why they developed the way they did.

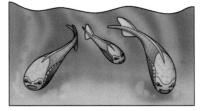

500 million years ago, the first fish evolved. They had thick skin and no jaws. There were no land animals at this time.

375 million years ago, some water-dwelling creatures began to leave the water, possibly to escape from predators. They were the first amphibians.

The fossil record

All the fossils found so far are together known as the fossil record. The fossil record shows us how plants and animals have changed over time. According to the fossil record, the first living things were bacteria, which first existed over 3,500 million years ago. Over the course of millions of years, these living things developed to become the first plants and animals.

300 million years ago, the first reptiles appeared. Their bodies were suited to life on land. They had dry, scaly skin to protect them from the Sun.

Around 240 million years ago, some reptiles evolved legs that supported their bodies from underneath. These were the first dinosaurs.

These are fossils of trilobites, which were among the first animals to have skeletons. They are around 550 million years old.

Internet link

For a link to an interactive website where you can play games to find out how different species evolved, go to www.usborne-quicklinks.com

38

A changing world

Living things change over time because environments change. Animals that are suited to the changes survive, while others die. The surviving animals pass on their useful qualities to their offspring. This is known as natural selection. Evidence for this also comes from animals alive today. Many types of animals that live in cold climates, for example, have adapted to their environment by evolving thick fur coats to help keep them warm.

Polar bears live in the freezing Arctic. They have evolved thick fur coats to help them survive in icy waters.

Shapes and sizes

The movement of the continents affected how dinosaurs evolved. During the Triassic period, when the continents were joined together as Pangaea, dinosaurs looked very similar worldwide. As the continents broke up, dinosaurs gradually developed different shapes and sizes to suit their new environments.

This fossilized skeleton of the ankylosaur Gastonia shows its defensive bony plates and spikes. Some of its spikes grew up to 1m (3ft) long.

Evolving features

Some dinosaur features evolved in response to other animals in the environment. Ankylosaurs, for example, gradually evolved bony plates and spikes as protection against meat-eating dinosaurs. Scientists think dinosaurs also evolved certain features to help them reproduce. Horned dinosaurs, such as Pentaceratops and Chasmosaurus, may have evolved the horns on their heads to help them attract mates.

Mass extinction

At the end of the Cretaceous period, there was a mass extinction of life on Earth. On land, all animals over 2m (7ft) long died out, and 70% of marine life became extinct. No dinosaurs survived the extinction. Scientists are still trying to work out why this happened.

Mesozoic mystery

Little evidence remains to show what really happened 65 million years ago. Most scientists think that an asteroid impact killed the dinosaurs, although others argue that climate change or volcanic eruptions may have wiped them out.

The evidence

To discover more about what caused the mass extinction, scientists study rocks that date from the time between the end of the Cretaceous period, 65 million years ago, and the beginning of the Tertiary period. As "K" is the symbol for the Cretaceous period and "T" is the symbol for the Tertiary period, these rocks are said to form the K–T boundary.

🦕 Internet link

For a link to a website that lists the main extinction theories and explains the reasoning behind them, go to www.usborne-quicklinks.com

This volcano in Hawaii is erupting runny lava capable of spreading for miles. Eruptions like this at the end of the Cretaceous period would have caused widespread devastation.

Lava floods

At the end of the Cretaceous period, there was an increase in volcanic activity around the world. In India, for example, massive volcanoes were spewing out floods of lava. The lava floods hardened into rock, and can be seen today at the K–T boundary known as the Deccan Traps.

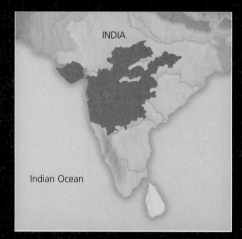

INDIA

Indian Ocean

The Deccan Traps (shaded in red) cover an area of nearly 500,000 sq km (195,000 sq miles) in western India.

Death by volcanoes

The floods of lava would have destroyed dinosaur habitats, as well as killing any dinosaurs in their path. The poisonous gases belched out by the volcanoes were even more dangerous. They may even have affected baby dinosaurs growing in their eggs. Gases from volcanoes can also alter the climate. Scientists think the gases may have made the climate either too warm or too cold for some dinosaur species to survive.

This shows how the asteroid may have looked as it collided with Earth. It would have burned up as it plummeted through the Earth's atmosphere, creating a fiery glow.

Disaster strikes

Around the time the dinosaurs died out, a huge asteroid, 10km (6 miles) wide, collided with the Earth. Scientists think they have found the giant crater it made at Chicxulub, in Mexico. Further evidence of an asteroid impact comes from particles of the metal iridium in K–T rocks around the world. Iridium is very rare on Earth, but is commonly found in asteroids.

Deadly impact

The effects of a large asteroid impact would have been deadly enough to kill the dinosaurs. The impact would have scattered molten debris across the planet's surface, starting global fires. It could also have set off a chain of devastating earthquakes and volcanic eruptions. Clouds of dust would have blocked out the sunlight, bringing global darkness and freezing conditions for many years.

The survivors

Not all life was wiped out by the K–T mass extinction. Small lizards, birds, insects, mammals and snakes survived whatever it was that killed the dinosaurs. Scientists are still unsure why some animals survived and others did not.

Small survivors

Scientists think one of the reasons smaller animals may have survived the mass extinction was because of their feeding habits. Smaller animals tend to eat a variety of food, whereas larger animals often rely on one specific food source. If that food source is wiped out, then the animals are faced with extinction.

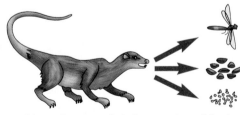

Mesozoic mammals fed on a variety of food, such as insects, nuts or seeds. This helped them to survive.

Large, meat-eating dinosaurs only fed on plant-eating dinosaurs. As soon as that food source was wiped out, the meat-eaters became extinct.

New life

Every mass extinction of life on Earth has been followed by a major burst of evolution. The Permian period, which preceded the Mesozoic era, ended in the mass extinction of up to 95% of all species. This extinction led to the evolution of the dinosaurs. The death of the dinosaurs left room for other animal groups to take over. This time mammals and birds spread over the world and developed into many different species.

Animals alive in the Mesozoic	K–T boundary	Surviving animals
Dinosaurs		
Pterosaurs		
Plesiosaurs		
Ammonites		
Mammals		
Crocodiles		
Lizards and snakes		
Turtles		
Amphibians		
Sharks and fishes		
Insects		
Birds		

This chart shows some of the animal groups that became extinct at the end of the Mesozoic era and some that survived.

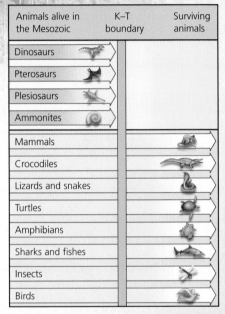

Megazostrodon lived around 180 million years ago and was typical of early mammals. It was only around 10cm (4in) long and probably fed on insects.

Mesozoic mammals

Mammals first appeared around 203 million years ago, but they were dwarfed by the dinosaurs. The first mammals were able to survive because they were small and came out mainly at night. Unlike the dinosaurs, mammals changed very little during the Mesozoic era and for more than 100 million years they stayed very small.

Rise of the mammals

After the death of the dinosaurs, mammals gradually evolved to occupy almost every habitat. One group of insect-eaters evolved into bats, developing flaps of skin between their long fingers, which enabled them to fly. Some land mammals moved into the oceans and developed streamlined bodies suited to life in the water. Mammals also took advantage of the different food sources available. Some mammals remained insect-eaters, while others adapted to feed on plants or other animals.

Human beings

One group of mammals, called primates, lived in trees. Over millions of years the primates evolved into apes, and then into human beings. Human beings have now been around for 2.3 million years. Compared to dinosaurs, which lived for 175 million years, humans have been on Earth for a very short period of time.

This baby chimpanzee is swinging through the branches using its superbly adapted hands and feet. Chimpanzees are part of the ape family, which first appeared on this planet around 30 million years ago.

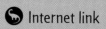 Internet link

For a link to a website where you can see amazing images of prehistoric animals, go to **www.usborne-quicklinks.com**

43

Dinosaur descendants

By comparing the skeleton of the oldest-known bird with the skeletons of small, theropod dinosaurs, scientists have now discovered that birds are directly descended from dinosaurs. Birds and dinosaurs have so many features in common that many scientists call birds "avian dinosaurs".

Common features

Scientists think birds evolved from a group of dinosaurs called dromaeosaurs, which had many bird-like features, including hollow bones and long feathery arms.

Dromaeosaurs and birds also share similar wrist joints. In dromaeosaurs, the wrist joints enabled them to fold their hands close to their arms, possibly to protect the feathers on their hands. Birds do a similar folding action as part of their flight stroke.

These diagrams show how, through a series of small changes, dinosaurs gradually evolved into birds.

★ Dromaeosaurs evolved feathers on their bodies, and especially long feathers on their arms.

The feathered arms developed into wings. Early birds had teeth, like dinosaurs, and heavy bodies. Most could fly.

Today's birds don't have teeth. Their bodies are much lighter, which helps them to fly better.

Early bird

The oldest-known bird is Archaeopteryx, which is from the late Jurassic period. Scientists look at Archaeopteryx as the midway point between dinosaurs and birds. Like dinosaurs, Archaeopteryx had a long, bony tail, sharp teeth and long fingers with curved claws. However, its feathers were more similar to the feathers of modern birds and were developed enough for flight.

This is a fossil of Archaeopteryx. It is about 150 million years old and was found in Solnhofen, Germany.

Missing links

Fossils such as Confuciusornis, a Cretaceous bird from China, show how the dinosaur-like birds of the Mesozoic gradually evolved into modern birds. Unlike modern birds, Confuciusornis had claws on its wings and it lacked the fan-like tail feathers seen on birds today. It had large toes, like modern birds', which would have helped it to perch on trees. Confuciusornis is also the earliest-known bird to have a toothless beak.

Male confuciusornithids had two long tail feathers, which they may have used to attract mates.

Learning to fly

Scientists are not sure how birds first took to the air and flew. Some think birds may have evolved wings to help them glide from tree to tree, and then developed the ability to flap their wings. Another theory suggests birds learnt to fly while running along the ground and leaping up to catch prey. The latest idea is that birds first flew as they beat their wings to help them get up slopes.

Successful species

There are billions of birds alive today, with over 9,000 different species. Birds are one of the most numerous and diverse groups of animals. It is amazing to think they are all descended from small, theropod dinosaurs.

Early birds may have leapt up to catch insects and then been lifted off the ground by a breeze.

🐾 Internet link

For a link to a website where you can read about the eight Archaeopteryx fossils found so far, go to
www.usborne-quicklinks.com

By flapping their wings, birds are able to power themselves up steep slopes. Early birds may have learned how to fly while doing this.

This is a hoatzin chick. Like Archaeopteryx and Confuciusornis, hoatzin chicks have claws on their wings. They are the only living birds to have claws on their wings.

Canyonlands National Park, Utah, USA. Over millions of years the many rivers that run through the canyon have carved the rock into amazing forms, as well as exposing vast areas of Mesozoic rock.

Dinosaurs by continent

Here you can find out where dinosaurs have been discovered around the world. You can read about the top dinosaur sites on each continent and some of the most famous and amazing dinosaur finds.

Looking for dinosaurs

Dinosaur bones have been found all over the world, from the dry Gobi Desert in Mongolia to the frozen plains of Alaska. Scientists are always looking for more dinosaurs, to find out more about them and to discover new ones. Around ten new species of dinosaurs are discovered around the world each year.

> **Internet link**
>
> For a link to a website where you can find out how a team of researchers has located fossil sites using satellite images, go to www.usborne-quicklinks.com

Giant humans and terrible lizards

For hundreds of years, people discovered dinosaur fossils without knowing what they were. Some people thought they were dragon bones, while others thought they belonged to elephants. An Englishman named Robert Plot even argued that a gigantic dinosaur thigh bone belonged to a giant human.

Then in 1842, a scientist named Richard Owen studied some giant reptile fossils. He realized that they were not related to any modern reptiles but made up a group of their own. He named the group Dinosauria, which means "terrible lizard".

This strange hollow is an imprint of a sauropod's thigh bone in Jurassic rocks in Colorado, USA. Perhaps it is not so surprising that before people knew dinosaurs existed, the discovery of such huge fossils led to some extraordinary theories about them.

Worldwide dinosaurs

At first, the main area where people hunted for dinosaurs was western North America. More dinosaur fossils have been found there than anywhere else in the world. But this could soon change, as scientists are beginning to spend more time and money looking for dinosaurs in southern parts of the world, such as Argentina and Madagascar. In the 1980s, dinosaurs were even found as far south as Antarctica, so dinosaurs have now been found on every continent on Earth.

Dinosaur Provincial Park, Canada
Hell Creek, USA
Dinosaur National Monument, USA
Southern England
Bernissart, Belgium
Gobi Desert, Mongolia
Liaoning, China
Sichuan, China
Bahariya Oasis, Egypt
Tendaguru, Tanzania
Mahajunga Basin, Madagascar
Valley of the Moon, Argentina
Neuquén, Argentina
Karoo Basin, South Africa
Dinosaur Cove, Australia

The red squares on this map show some of the main sites around the world where dinosaurs have been found.

This satellite image shows the Gobi Desert from space. It is useful to paleontologists as it gives them an accurate view of the area.

This image is of the same area, but the different shades highlight different types of rock and vegetation. The purple area marks a potential dinosaur site.

Searching from space

Developments in technology mean that paleontologists can now predict where dinosaurs may be found with even greater accuracy. When working in vast areas, they use satellite images to pinpoint potential dinosaur sites. Heat detectors on satellites can detect different types of land surfaces. For example, they can pick out sedimentary rock where dinosaur fossils may be found. The information from the heat detectors shows up in different shades on the satellite image.

Naming new dinosaurs

Each new dinosaur is given a name, either by the person who discovered it or by the paleontologists who identified it. Most names are made up of Latin and Greek words. Sometimes, a dinosaur is given a name that describes something unusual about its features. For example, Stegosaurus means "plated lizard". It gets its name from the plates on its back. Other dinosaurs are named after the place where they were found or after a person. However, scientists are not allowed to name dinosaurs after themselves. You can find out what the different dinosaur names mean on pages 118–133.

Incisivosaurus, a strange-looking dinosaur from China, was discovered in 2002. It was named after the bizarre buck-teeth at the front of its mouth, as Incisivosaurus means "incisor lizard" (incisors are front teeth).

South America

Some of the most exciting dinosaur finds in South America have come from Argentina. They include some of the oldest dinosaur fossils found so far.

Small beginnings

The discovery of Triassic dinosaurs in South America showed scientists what early dinosaurs were like. Staurikosaurus and Pisanosaurus, for example, were both small, quick-moving and walked on two legs.

Getting bigger

The first large dinosaurs were the prosauropods. They appeared in South America at the end of the Triassic period and their remains have been found in many parts of the world. Riojasaurus, a 10m (33ft) long prosauropod from Argentina, would have been one of the largest dinosaurs of its time.

Riojasaurus was a plant-eater with a small head and a bulky body. It lived around 210 million years ago.

The dinosaur symbols on this map show where those dinosaurs have been found. The black squares mark two of the major dinosaur sites in South America.

An important site where scientists discovered some of the largest dinosaurs. See pages 54–55.

Some of the earliest dinosaurs were found here. Read more about them on pages 52–53.

VENEZUELA

FRENCH GUIANA

GUYANA

SURINAM

Antarctosaurus

COLOMBIA

ECUADOR

BRAZIL

PERU

BOLIVIA

PARAGUAY

Saltasaurus

Riojasaurus

CHILE   ARGENTINA

Staurikosaurus

Antarctosaurus

Laplatasaurus

URUGUAY

■ The Valley of the Moon

■ Nuequén

Patagosaurus

Volkheimeria

Piatnitzkysaurus

Rare remains

Fewer Jurassic dinosaurs have been found in South America than on other continents. So far, all of the Jurassic finds come from Argentina. They include the large sauropods Patagosaurus and Volkheimeria, and the theropod Piatnitzkysaurus, which probably preyed on them. However, there could be many more, as paleontologists have only recently begun to look for dinosaurs in South America.

Santanaraptor

Irritator

Gondwanatitan

Patagosaurus probably tried to defend itself against attackers by kicking out with its powerful front legs.

Piatnitzkysaurus was only about a third of the size of Patagosaurus, but it was probably capable of attacking the much larger animal.

Irritators had long, thin snouts, which would have helped them to catch fish. Their sharp teeth enabled them to grip their catch well.

Gondwana dinosaurs

Scientists used to think that Gondwana broke up in the early Cretaceous period, but they now believe that South America and Africa were still connected in the middle of the period. In 1996, a mid-Cretaceous spinosaur named Irritator was discovered in Brazil. Mid-Cretaceous spinosaurs are also known from Africa, so the two continents must still have been joined at that time for the spinosaurs to have spread between them.

🦕 Internet link

For a link to a website where you can find out more about the dinosaurs that have been found in South America, go to www.usborne-quicklinks.com

The Valley of the Moon

The Valley of the Moon, in Argentina, got its name from the strange moon-like landscape of bare, jagged rock and deep valleys. Some of the oldest dinosaur fossils have been found there: Herrerasaurus, Pisanosaurus and Eoraptor. They lived around 225 million years ago.

Changing landscape

Today, the Valley of the Moon has very little plant-life and is dry and dusty. But, 225 million years ago there were large rivers and it rained frequently. The rivers often overflowed, flooding the surrounding land. Huge fossilized tree trunks more than 40m (130ft) tall have been found in the area, suggesting it was covered in forests.

The Valley of the Moon, shaded in red, covers an area of 250 sq km (97 sq miles) in northwest Argentina.

Triassic fossils

Most of the fossils from the Valley of the Moon are not dinosaurs at all, but crocodile-like archosaurs, which were the dominant predators of the time. The largest of these was Saurosuchus, a ferocious predator, with huge jaws and teeth, that grew up to 7m (23ft) long. Its heavy body and short legs made it slower than the dinosaurs.

This picture of Saurosuchus shows how short its legs were compared to the size of its body.

★

This is the Valley of the Moon today. The strange rock formations, called hoodoos, have been shaped by the strong winds that blow through the valley.

Tiny dinosaur

The smallest dinosaur from the Valley of the Moon was a meat-eater named Eoraptor, which was only 1m (3ft) long. Although Eoraptor was a predator, its size probably meant that it had to spend most of its time avoiding other animals. It fed on small reptiles and insects, but it may have eaten plants as well. At the back of its mouth it had sharp teeth for tearing meat, and at the front it had more rounded teeth, which it may have used to strip leaves off plants.

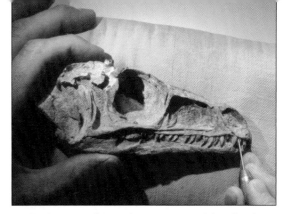

A scientist uses a fine tool to remove particles of rock from Eoraptor's skull. Eoraptor had such a small skull that extra care had to be taken to prepare its delicate bones.

Designed to hunt

Herrerasaurus was one of the largest meat-eating dinosaurs of its time. It had many features that made it a successful killer, including sharp claws and unusually long teeth in its upper jaws. Its long back legs meant it could run fast too. Herrerasaurus probably preyed on the plant-eating Pisanosaurus, Eoraptor and other reptiles.

> 🦕 **Internet link**
>
> For a link to a website where you can find out more about the Valley of the Moon and see photographs of its amazing rock formations, go to **www.usborne-quicklinks.com**

Herrerasaurus walked on two legs, so it was free to use the sharp claws on its hands to grapple with its prey.

Land of the giants

In Neuquén, an area in southwest Argentina, scientists have found fossils of some of the largest dinosaurs. These include members of the sauropod group the titanosaurs, and Giganotosaurus, one of the fiercest predators.

Rivers to deserts

Today, much of Neuquén is desert, but in the late Cretaceous period there were wide rivers and dry, open woodland. It must have been covered in rich vegetation, to support the enormous plant-eating titanosaurs.

Enormous titanosaur

The largest titanosaur, Argentinosaurus, was also one of the largest dinosaurs. It was about the height of a building with five floors. Like other titanosaurs, Argentinosaurus had bony lumps of skin on its back, ranging from the size of a pea to about the size of a human fist. These lumps helped to protect Argentinosaurus from attacks by other dinosaurs.

Few dinosaurs would have been big enough to attack Argentinosaurus. Its main predator was probably Giganotosaurus, the largest theropod in the area.

Terrifying claws

In 1998, a giant toe claw was discovered in Neuquén. The claw belonged to a new dinosaur, which scientists named Megaraptor. Scientists think Megaraptor was a quick-moving and deadly predator which used the long claws on its toes to slice open its prey. Based on the length of the claw, scientists estimate that Megaraptor grew over 8m (26ft) long.

Megaraptor's speed and deadly claws meant that it could easily catch and kill other dinosaurs. Its most lethal weapon was the especially long claw on its second toe, which was 35cm (14in) long.

Giant meat-eater

Giganotosaurus was one of the largest land predators. It was about 12.5m (41ft) long and 4m (13ft) tall. Giganotosaurus belonged to a group called the carcharodontosaurs, which were among the fiercest meat-eaters in Africa and South America during the Cretaceous period.

Slashing teeth

Most of Giganotosaurus' skeleton has been found, including the skull and teeth. Its teeth were large and blade-like, and were well suited to slicing through flesh. Giganotosaurus probably attacked its prey by biting them repeatedly until they bled to death.

Scientists think giganotosaurs may have lived together in groups.

🌐 **Internet link**

For a link to a website where you can see amazing skeletons of Argentinosaurus and Giganotosaurus, go to www.usborne-quicklinks.com

North America

North America is a dinosaur hunter's dream. It has some of the richest fossil sites in the world, and is home to famous dinosaurs such as Triceratops and Stegosaurus, neither of which has been found anywhere else in the world.

Spreading seas

In the Cretaceous period, a shallow sea formed in North America and gradually spread, separating the eastern and western halves of the continent. The east was still connected to Europe, but western North America became an island, with its own dinosaur types. Instead of sauropods, which dominated other parts of the world, western North America had large numbers of hadrosaurs, tyrannosaurs and ceratopsians.

Asian relatives

Although western North America was an island, at some points in the Cretaceous period there seems to have been a land bridge linking it with eastern Asia. Each time the sea level dropped and the bridge was uncovered, dinosaurs crossed it. As a result, some east Asian dinosaurs closely resemble North American species.

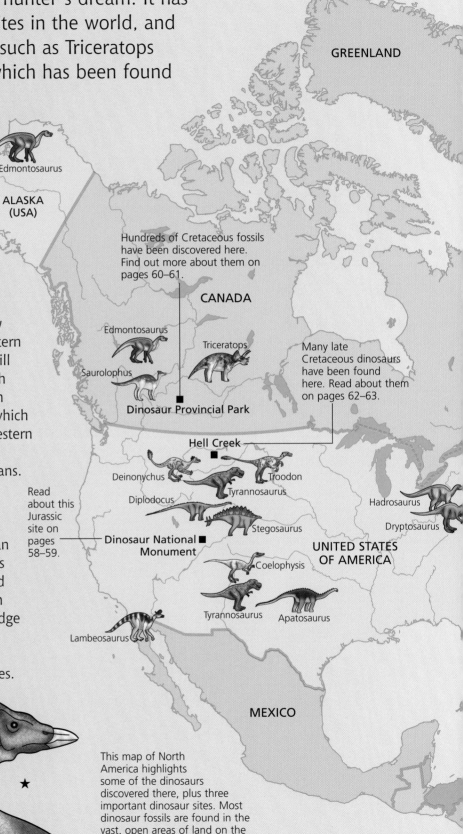

GREENLAND

ALASKA (USA)

Edmontosaurus

Hundreds of Cretaceous fossils have been discovered here. Find out more about them on pages 60–61.

CANADA

Edmontosaurus

Triceratops

Saurolophus

Many late Cretaceous dinosaurs have been found here. Read about them on pages 62–63.

Dinosaur Provincial Park

Hell Creek

Deinonychus

Troodon

Diplodocus

Tyrannosaurus

Hadrosaurus

Read about this Jurassic site on pages 58–59.

Dinosaur National Monument

Stegosaurus

Dryptosaurus

UNITED STATES OF AMERICA

Coelophysis

Tyrannosaurus

Apatosaurus

Lambeosaurus

MEXICO

This map of North America highlights some of the dinosaurs discovered there, plus three important dinosaur sites. Most dinosaur fossils are found in the vast, open areas of land on the western side of the continent.

Saurolophus lived in both Asia and North America. This illustration shows an American Saurolophus (far right) and its Asian relative. They look similar, but the Asian species has a longer crest.

Primitive predator

In 1947, more than a hundred well-preserved Coelophysis skeletons were found by paleontologists working on an area of land known as Ghost Ranch, in northern New Mexico. The skeletons show that Coelophysis was a lightly-built theropod, no bigger than 3m (10ft) long when fully grown. It is one of the most primitive theropods ever found.

This is a Coelophysis from Ghost Ranch. Baby Coelophysis bones were found near its ribs, suggesting that it had eaten its own young. However, new research shows that the adult is lying on top of the baby.

Killing machines

One of the last giant meat-eating dinosaurs, Tyrannosaurus, lived in North America between 70 and 65 million years ago. It was a massive beast with excellent sight and hearing, which would have helped it to track down prey. Its legs were strong, so it could probably run very fast over short distances. However, its arms were tiny and their function is a mystery. They were too short to have lifted food to the tyrannosaur's mouth and, although muscular, were probably too small to be of much use when fighting.

Internet link

For a link to a website where you can read about "Sue", the most complete Tyrannosaurus skeleton ever found, go to www.usborne-quicklinks.com

Rival tyrannosaurs would have fought by lunging at each others' necks or heads. Scientists know this because many Tyrannosaurus skulls have bite marks in them from other tyrannosaurs.

Jurassic graveyard

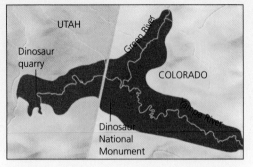

UTAH

Dinosaur quarry

Green River

COLORADO

Dinosaur National Monument

Green River

The Dinosaur National Monument, shaded in red, covers 800 sq km (310 sq miles). It contains a large quarry where many dinosaur fossils have been found.

The Dinosaur National Monument in Colorado and Utah, USA, is the most diverse late Jurassic site in the world. Hundreds of sauropod bones have been uncovered there, and other notable finds include many Stegosaurus remains and a few well-preserved theropod skeletons.

A watery grave

The area now called the Dinosaur National Monument had a large dinosaur population in Jurassic times, mainly because there were many rivers to drink from. The land was flat, so the rivers flooded in rainy periods. In each flood, any dead dinosaurs were swept away and deposited at bends in the river where the current slowed. They were buried in sediment and gradually fossilized.

Paleontologists have now discovered many of these bones in the Monument's dinosaur quarry. Visitors to the quarry can admire its fossil wall, where more than 1,500 bones are embedded in a steep rock face.

A paleontologist chips away at a section of the Monument's fossil wall, revealing many more dinosaur bones.

Long-tailed giants

Four types of sauropods have been found at the Monument: Apatosaurus, Barosaurus, Camarasaurus and Diplodocus. Diplodocus is one of the longest dinosaurs ever discovered, and its tail alone could be as long as 14m (46ft). The large tail bones were hollow and relatively light, so Diplodocus could hold its tail up as it walked. There is evidence for this in its fossil tracks, which have no drag marks from the tail.

Some of Diplodocus' tail bones are flat underneath. This suggests that the dinosaur sometimes leaned back on its tail.

★ This illustration shows how Diplodocus may have used its long tail for support when rearing up to feed from high branches.

Jurassic predator

North America's most common late Jurassic meat-eater was Allosaurus. A nearly perfect Allosaurus skull found at the Monument has more than 70 sharp, serrated teeth that would have sliced easily through flesh. The skull also has evidence of large jaw muscles that would have allowed Allosaurus to open its mouth extra-wide. Deep Allosaurus bite marks have been found in many huge sauropod bones, indicating that this fierce predator was capable of attacking dinosaurs up to ten times its size.

Allosaurus frequently attacked large plant-eaters such as Stegosaurus. Although Stegosaurus defended itself by whipping its spiked tail, Allosaurus was likely to win the fight.

Sturdy stegosaur

Stegosaurus is the largest stegosaur ever found. It was a common herbivore in North America during the Jurassic period. It had two rows of large, bony plates on its neck, back and tail. These plates, which would have been covered with skin, were full of blood vessels and helped to control the dinosaur's body temperature.

To keep warm, Stegosaurus let the Sun shine directly onto its wide, flat plates, like this. The plates absorbed the Sun's heat.

Hot plates

To warm its body, Stegosaurus stood with its plates facing the Sun. The Sun's rays warmed the blood flowing through the plates, which then spread around the body. If Stegosaurus wanted to cool down, it stood in the shade, so the plates lost heat instead.

Stegosaurus may have been able to pump extra blood into its plates, making them flush bright red. This would have made the plates look more intimidating to enemies, or perhaps more attractive to potential mates.

Diplodocus' neck was about 8m (26ft) long. It was normally held in a horizontal position, but could be raised briefly to reach high branches.

Internet link

For a link to a website where you can take on the role of Big Al the Allosaurus and test your survival skills, go to www.usborne-quicklinks.com

Dinosaur park

Dinosaur Provincial Park, in southern Alberta, Canada, contains some of the most important fossil discoveries ever made. Paleontologists at the park have uncovered more than 300 well-preserved skeletons of late Cretaceous dinosaurs.

Dinosaur Provincial Park is a large expanse of dry, rocky land. Severe erosion has created many hoodoos, like this one.

An ideal home

In the Cretaceous period, southern Alberta was covered in thick vegetation. This meant that plant-eating dinosaurs thrived there, as did dinosaur predators, which found plenty of prey. At least 35 dinosaur species have been discovered in the park so far, including large numbers of ceratopsians, hadrosaurs and tyrannosaurs.

Deadly stampede

One of the most impressive discoveries in the park is a fossil bed containing bones of a huge herd of centrosaurs. Scientists think that tens of thousands of migrating centrosaurs may have tried to cross a flooded river, and drowned in the process. Many of the bones are broken and crushed, suggesting that as some animals stumbled and fell, others trampled them in the panic to get across.

Dinosaur Provincial Park covers 73 sq km (28 sq miles) of land near the Rocky Mountains.

This scene shows a group of centrosaurs about to cross a river. Centrosaurs probably migrated in herds like this each summer, heading north, where the temperature was milder.

Hadrosaurs such as Parasaurolophus (left) and Corythosaurus (right) lived in Alberta. Different species ate different plants, so they could live close together without competing for food.

🦕 Internet link

For a link to a website where you can find out about the work of paleontologists in the Dinosaur Provincial Park and read field reports from the last few years, go to www.usborne-quicklinks.com

Fearsome predator

The meat-eater Albertosaurus was a smaller relative of Tyrannosaurus. It lived in North America between 75 and 70 million years ago. The first Albertosaurus fossil, a skull, came from Alberta, which is how the dinosaur got its name. Scientists have since discovered several Albertosaurus skeletons together. This suggests that they roamed, and maybe hunted, in groups.

Honking hadrosaurs

Hadrosaurs were very common in North America in the Cretaceous period, and bones of more than five different species have been found in the Dinosaur Provincial Park. Some hadrosaurs had hollow, bony crests on their heads. They may have been able to blow air through the crest to make a loud, bellowing noise. As they lived in herds, they probably produced this honking sound to warn other hadrosaurs of danger.

Albertosaurus had an enormous skull, which was deeper and broader than those of other tyrannosaurs.

★

This is a diagram of a Parasaurolophus skull, showing the air passages in its hollow crest. The dinosaur blew up through its nostrils to make a noise.

This is a Lambeosaurus crest. Different crest shapes probably produced different sounds, and each hadrosaur would have recognized the calls of its own species.

Hell Creek

The area known as Hell Creek lies just east of the Rocky Mountains, in Montana, USA. The land there has been eroded to reveal late Cretaceous rocks, which contain remains of some of the very last dinosaurs.

Hell Creek is an arid region of land in eastern Montana, USA, near the Canadian border.

A Cretaceous plain

Many dinosaurs lived in Hell Creek between 70 and 65 million years ago. At that time, the land was a wide, low-lying plain, crossed by many rivers. The climate was mild, with high rainfall, which produced plenty of vegetation for herbivores.

Butting boneheads

Many pachycephalosaurs, or bone-headed dinosaurs, lived in North America in the late Cretaceous period. The largest was Pachycephalosaurus, which had a domed skull up to 25cm (10in) thick. It probably used its hard head as a battering ram, charging at rival males when competing for mates. It was able to hold its back and tail rigid when butting, so that the shock of the impact didn't dislocate its spine.

This Pachycephalosaurus skull has bony spikes around its domed top. These were probably intended both to intimidate enemies and attract mates.

Pachycephalosaurs fought by butting each other's bodies. Scientists used to think that they crashed their heads together, but now believe that the impact would have shattered their skulls.

King of Hell Creek

The first ever Tyrannosaurus skeleton was found at Hell Creek in 1902, and since then more have been uncovered nearby. Tyrannosaurus seems to have been the only large theropod in the area, and would have preyed on Hell Creek's many plant-eaters. Tyrannosaurus teeth marks have been found in the bones of different dinosaurs, including hadrosaurs and ceratopsians.

Three-horned head

Triceratops, the largest ceratopsian, was very common in North America in the late Cretaceous. Its name means "three-horned face", referring to its two long eyebrow horns and shorter snout horn. Triceratops may have used these to stab at enemies, perhaps charging at them like a rhinoceros does. It also had a solid, bony frill that protected the neck when the head was raised. It probably displayed the frill to attract mates, by lowering its head so that the frill stood straight up.

After catching its prey, Tyrannosaurus ripped off chunks of flesh and bone. Its teeth were so strong that it could crunch up the animal's bones and swallow them along with the meat.

Triceratops' skull made up about one-third of the dinosaur's total length. Its horns were even longer when the animal was alive, as each was covered with a thick, horny layer that has not fossilized.

Internet link

For a link to a website where you can look at photographs of a dig at Hell Creek where Triceratops and hadrosaur bones were found, go to **www.usborne-quicklinks.com**

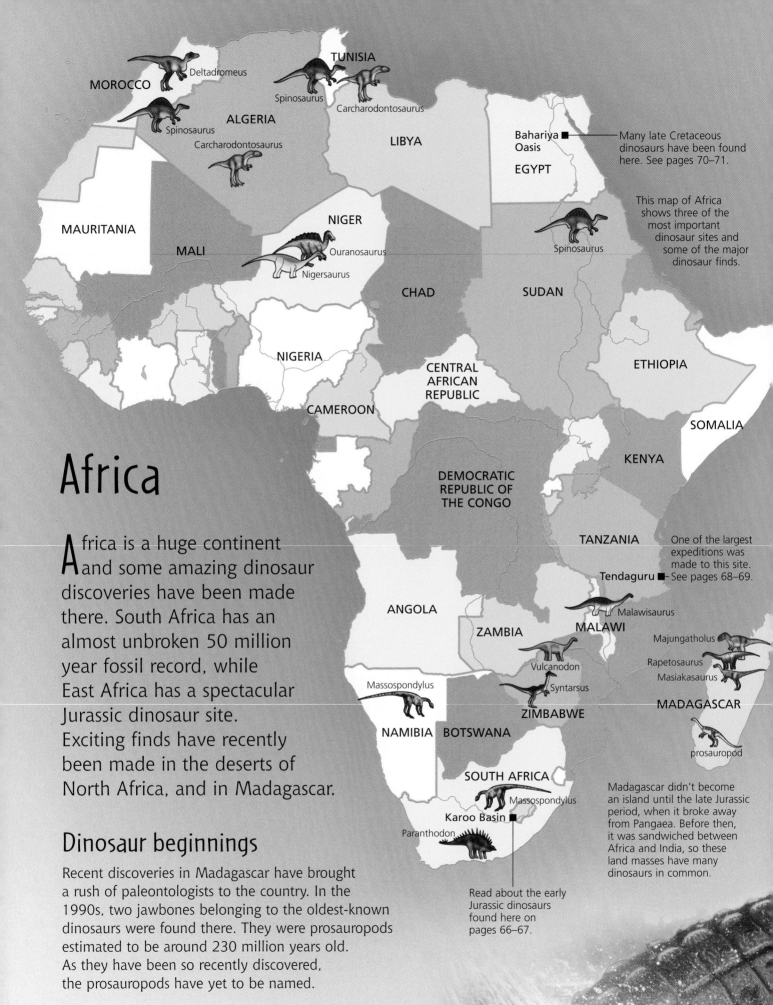

Africa

Africa is a huge continent and some amazing dinosaur discoveries have been made there. South Africa has an almost unbroken 50 million year fossil record, while East Africa has a spectacular Jurassic dinosaur site. Exciting finds have recently been made in the deserts of North Africa, and in Madagascar.

Dinosaur beginnings

Recent discoveries in Madagascar have brought a rush of paleontologists to the country. In the 1990s, two jawbones belonging to the oldest-known dinosaurs were found there. They were prosauropods estimated to be around 230 million years old. As they have been so recently discovered, the prosauropods have yet to be named.

Deltadromeus

MOROCCO

TUNISIA

Spinosaurus

Carcharodontosaurus

ALGERIA

Spinosaurus

Carcharodontosaurus

LIBYA

Baharilya Oasis

EGYPT

Many late Cretaceous dinosaurs have been found here. See pages 70–71.

MAURITANIA

MALI

NIGER

Ouranosaurus

Nigersaurus

This map of Africa shows three of the most important dinosaur sites and some of the major dinosaur finds.

Spinosaurus

CHAD

SUDAN

NIGERIA

CENTRAL AFRICAN REPUBLIC

ETHIOPIA

CAMEROON

DEMOCRATIC REPUBLIC OF THE CONGO

SOMALIA

KENYA

TANZANIA

One of the largest expeditions was made to this site. See pages 68–69.

Tendaguru

ANGOLA

ZAMBIA

MALAWI

Malawisaurus

Majungatholus

Rapetosaurus

Masiakasaurus

MADAGASCAR

Massospondylus

Vulcanodon

Syntarsus

ZIMBABWE

NAMIBIA

BOTSWANA

prosauropod

Madagascar didn't become an island until the late Jurassic period, when it broke away from Pangaea. Before then, it was sandwiched between Africa and India, so these land masses have many dinosaurs in common.

SOUTH AFRICA

Massospondylus

Karoo Basin

Paranthodon

Read about the early Jurassic dinosaurs found here on pages 66–67.

Strange sails

Many of the dinosaurs from North Africa had bony spines on their backs, which supported a sail of skin. Scientists are not sure what the sails were for. They may have been used to attract mates or to help make the dinosaurs look more aggressive. Some scientists think that the sails may have been used in the same way as stegosaurs' plates, to help keep the dinosaurs' bodies at the right temperature.

★

Male ouranosaurs may have had brighter sails than females, and used their sails to attract mates.

🐾 **Internet link**

For a link to a website where you can read about what Africa was like 100 million years ago, go to www.usborne-quicklinks.com

Mesozoic lawnmower

One of the most unusual dinosaurs from North Africa is Nigersaurus, a sauropod that lived 100 to 90 million years ago. At 15m (49ft) long, Nigersaurus was a medium-sized sauropod, but it had incredibly wide jaws. These held around 600 needle-shaped teeth. Nigersaurus probably fed by swinging its neck across the ground and cropping plants with its teeth, like an enormous lawnmower. Almost all of Nigersaurus' skeleton has been found.

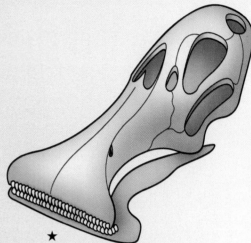

★

Nigersaurus' mouth is wider than any other dinosaur's found so far. Its jaws were much wider than its face.

Supercroc

A supercrocodile called Sarcosuchus lived at the same time and in the same area as Nigersaurus. Sarcosuchus was more than twice the size of any crocodile living today, and about ten times heavier. It had eyes on the very top of its head that could tilt up, so it could lie hidden in the water and watch for any animals passing by. Sarcosuchus probably preyed on dinosaurs and other large animals.

Sarcosuchus lay in wait along riverbanks and attacked victims, such as Nigersaurus, when they came to the river to drink.

Desert dinosaurs

The Karoo Basin is a vast, lowland area surrounded by mountains. It covers almost two-thirds of the surface of South Africa. In the early Jurassic period, it was a wide expanse of desert and the dinosaurs that lived there survived in hot, dry conditions.

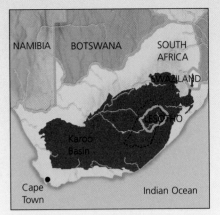

On this map of southern Africa, the Karoo Basin is shaded in red. The dinosaurs were found within the area marked by the dotted black line.

Karoo Basin

The Karoo Basin is made up of thick layers of sedimentary rock, which date from 240 to 190 million years ago. By looking at the types of rock in each layer, scientists are able to work out what the climate was like at the time. We know that the dinosaurs from the early Jurassic period lived in desert conditions, as the rocks from the Jurassic period are made up of tiny, wind-blown sand particles.

Internet link

For a link to a website where you can read about the fossils of reptiles found in the Karoo Basin, go to www.usborne-quicklinks.com

Shelter from the Sun

The dinosaurs from the Karoo were all relatively small. This may have been because small dinosaurs were better suited to living in the desert, as their size made it easier to find shelter from the Sun. The smallest dinosaur from the Karoo was Lesothosaurus, which was only about the size of a turkey.

Lesothosaurs probably lived in herds for protection against predators, such as the crested theropod Syntarsus.

This is the Karoo Basin. Today it is covered in grasses and woody shrubs.

Digging dinosaurs

Heterodontosaurus may have slept in burrows during the hottest part of the year.

★

Heterodontosaurus was another small, fast-moving dinosaur from the Karoo. It had three different kinds of teeth, for biting, tearing and grinding food. It also had long fingers and toes, and sharp, powerful claws, which meant that it was good at digging. Like many desert animals today, Heterodontosaurus may have sheltered from the Sun's heat by digging burrows in the sand.

King of the Karoo

At around 4m (13ft) long, the prosauropod Massospondylus was the largest dinosaur from the Karoo. However, most of its length was in its neck and tail, and its body was only about the size of a small pony. Massospondylus had especially large hands and feet, which would have helped it to dig for plants and roots, as well as any water underground.

Massospondylus had extremely large claws, which would have helped it to tear roots from the ground.

Cracks in the Karoo

The Karoo Basin once straddled the boundary between the African and the Antarctic plate. When Pangaea began to break up 190 million years ago, the two plates pulled apart and cracks appeared in the Karoo. Burning hot molten rock, or lava, rose up through the cracks, flooding 2 million sq km (0.8 million sq miles) of land. Most dinosaurs and other animals would have managed to escape the flooding and flee to other areas, but the lava would have destroyed their habitats and made it impossible for animals to live in the Karoo for many years.

The largest expedition

One of the biggest dinosaur expeditions ever was to Tendaguru, a remote hill in Tanzania, East Africa. The expedition lasted from 1909 until 1913 and involved around 900 people. Ten different kinds of dinosaurs, all from the late Jurassic period, were discovered there.

Tendaguru is in the south of Tanzania. All the dinosaur bones were shipped to Germany from Lindi, the nearest port.

Tons of bones

The Tendaguru expedition was organized by a team of German scientists. They employed local people to dig pits all over Tendaguru. The locals had to carry the bones to a nearby port, a four-day walk away, so they could be shipped to Germany. Over four years, 250 tonnes (275 tons) of bone were removed and nearly 5,000 trips were made between the site and the port.

Similar sites

Many of the different types of dinosaurs from Tendaguru have also been found at Dinosaur National Monument in Utah, North America. Africa and North America were joined in the late Jurassic period, so dinosaurs could spread between them. The theropods Allosaurus and Ceratosaurus, for example, are known from both sites. Only a few Ceratosaurus teeth were found at Tendaguru, but their size suggests they belonged to one of the largest species of Ceratosaurus.

Male ceratosaurs had sharp horns on their heads. Two rival males would fight by trying to butt each other with their horns.

🦕 Internet link

For a link to a website where you can read about the expedition to Tendaguru and find out what Tendaguru is like now, go to www.usborne-quicklinks.com

Death by drowning

Numerous bones of the stegosaur Kentrosaurus were found at Tendaguru. One ancient riverbed alone contained more than 70 Kentrosaurus thighbones, which may be from a herd drowned by a flash flood. Kentrosaurus was one of the spikiest stegosaurs, with seven tail spikes and another pair of spikes on its shoulders. It probably used its tail spikes to defend itself against large theropods, such as Ceratosaurus.

Tallest dinosaur

Five different kinds of sauropods were discovered at the site: Barosaurus, Dicraeosaurus, Janenschia, Tendaguria and Brachiosaurus. Brachiosaurus was the tallest dinosaur. Unlike other sauropods, it had front legs that were much longer than its hind legs. These raised its neck and shoulders high above the ground, enabling it to feed on leaves that no other dinosaurs could reach.

A Brachiosaurus could eat a lot of leaves in one mouthful. Their mouths were wide enough to swallow a human whole.

Amazing skeleton

The remains of several brachiosaurs were found at Tendaguru. By combining the bones of different individuals, scientists were able to put together a whole skeleton, which is now on display at the Humboldt Museum, in Berlin, Germany. It stands nearly 25m (82ft) long and 12m (39ft) high, and is the largest complete dinosaur skeleton in the world.

The lost dinosaurs of Egypt

This map of Egypt shows the Bahariya Oasis, the site where a number of late Cretaceous dinosaurs were found.

In the early 1900s, a German paleontologist named Ernst Stromer uncovered a mass of dinosaur bones in the Sahara Desert in Egypt. The fossils were taken to Germany and stored in a museum. In 1944, a Second World War bombing raid destroyed the museum and all the fossils Stromer had collected.

Lost bones

Stromer discovered the theropods Spinosaurus, Bahariasaurus and Carcharodontosaurus, and the titanosaur Aegyptosaurus. After the fossils were destroyed, everything scientists knew about these dinosaurs was based on Stromer's detailed descriptions.

Long-snouted spinosaur

Spinosaurus was the first spinosaur to be discovered. It had a long snout and straight, narrow teeth, similar to those of crocodiles. Like crocodiles, Spinosaurus had a varied diet. It probably ate fish as well as other dinosaurs. Spinosaurus was possibly the largest theropod. It grew up to 15m (49ft) long and had a huge sail on its back, which made it seem even larger.

Spinosaurus could keep its snout in water while fishing and still be able to breathe, as its nostrils were set back from the tip of its snout.

Shark-toothed dinosaur

All Stromer knew about Carcharodontosaurus was that it was a huge dinosaur and that it had large, triangular teeth like a shark's. Then in 1995, an enormous skull was found in Morocco.

The skull confirmed that Carcharodontosaurus was one of the largest meat-eating dinosaurs, and that it was closely related to Giganotosaurus, from South America. These two species may have shared a common ancestor that lived at a time when South America and Africa were joined, but when the continents broke apart, the two types of dinosaurs developed differently.

This Carcharodontosaurus skull is 1.5m (5ft) long. Carcharodontosaurus had incredibly sharp and powerful teeth, which would have helped it to slice through the flesh of other animals.

Swampy Sahara

In 2000, a team of paleontologists set out to rediscover Stromer's site at the Bahariya Oasis. As Stromer had not left behind any maps, they had to find the site by matching the landscape to Stromer's descriptions. Today, the Bahariya Oasis is hot, dry desert, but by studying the rocks there the expedition discovered that during the late Cretaceous period it had been swampland. A huge variety of animals lived there, including turtles, crocodiles and fish.

New discovery

The expedition also found fossils of a new titanosaur, Paralititan. It is the first new dinosaur to be discovered in Egypt since 1916 and may also be the second-largest dinosaur ever found. A single theropod tooth was found nearby. This suggests a theropod may have scavenged Paralititan's remains, or the tooth could be from a dinosaur that attacked and killed Paralititan.

Paralititan's arm bone was so heavy that it took seven members of the expedition to lift it from the ground.

Internet link

For a link to a website where you can find out more about Stromer's discoveries at Bahariya Oasis and look at photographs, go to www.usborne-quicklinks.com

Europe

D inosaurs probably lived all over Europe, but many countries are now so densely populated that it is hard to dig for fossils there. Nevertheless, Europe has a long tradition of dinosaur excavation and research.

🦕 Internet link

For a link to a website where you can see a list of the dinosaur fossils found in Europe, go to
www.usborne-quicklinks.com

Tropical swamp

In early Mesozoic times, Europe was hot and dry. Later, during the Cretaceous period, conditions became more tropical, and rivers, marshes and lush forests appeared. The landscape was probably much like the swampy Everglades area in Florida, USA, which is home to many modern reptiles. A wide range of dinosaurs lived in Cretaceous Europe, including ankylosaurs, hadrosaurs and sauropods.

This illustration shows a herd of plateosaurs coming to a river to drink. Many plateosaurs have been found in Germany, France and Switzerland.

Euro dino

A common European dinosaur was Plateosaurus, a long-necked prosauropod from the late Triassic period. Plateosaurus skeletons have been found at more than 50 locations across the continent. The biggest site is Trossingen, in Germany, where hundreds of well-preserved skeletons have been uncovered.

Dinosaurs have been found mainly in central and western Europe. Southern England in particular is rich in dinosaur remains. You can read more about these on pages 76–77.

Find out about the many dinosaurs from the Isle of Wight on pages 78–79.

Many Iguanodon skeletons were found in Bernissart, Belgium. Read more about this site on pages 74–75.

NORWAY

SWEDEI

IRELAND

UNITED KINGDOM

Megalosaurus

Scelidosaurus

Baryonyx

Bernissart

GERMANY

Iguanodon

Archaeopteryx

Plateosaurus

Compsogna

Plateosaurus

FRANCE

Plateosaurus

SWITZERLAND

Telmatosaurus

Compsognathus

Variraptor

ITALY

Pelecanimimus

PORTUGAL

Allosaurus

Iguanodon

Scipionyx

Hypsilophodon

Dacentrurus

SPAIN

Vicious Variraptor

Until recently, scientists thought that the dinosaur carnivores called dromaeosaurs had not lived in Europe. However, a few European dromaeosaur fragments have now been unearthed, including Variraptor, a late Cretaceous dromaeosaur found in France in 1998. Variraptor had strong arms and sharp teeth, as well as the long, curved toe claws common to dromaeosaurs.

Variraptors probably attacked in groups like this, leaping onto their prey and ripping its flesh with their long claws.

Hardly any dinosaur fossils have been found in northern and eastern Europe. This is due to a lack of exposed Mesozoic rock, as well as very limited dinosaur research in these areas.

FINLAND

ESTONIA

LATVIA

HUANIA

BELARUS

RUSSIA

UKRAINE

MOLDOVA

ROMANIA

Valdosaurus

Struthiosaurus

BULGARIA

TURKEY

GREECE

ND

Small and swift

Compsognathus was a tiny late Jurassic theropod. Only two Compsognathus skeletons have so far been found, both in Europe. One of them was discovered in Solnhofen, Germany, in 1859, and is almost perfectly preserved. Even its last meal, a lizard, is fossilized inside its ribcage.

This Compsognathus skeleton from Solnhofen, Germany, is almost complete. Its neck is bent over its back and its long tail and back legs stick out to the left.

Iguanodon mine

One of Europe's most significant dinosaur finds consisted of more than 30 complete Iguanodon skeletons. The bones were found in a Belgian coal mine and have made Iguanodon one of the world's most studied dinosaurs.

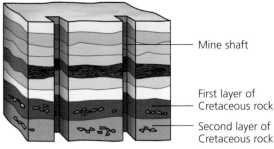

This is a diagram of the mine at Bernissart. The Iguanodon skeletons were found deep underground, in two separate layers of early Cretaceous rock.

A lucky find

The Iguanodon bones were discovered by chance, in 1878, when coal miners digging in western Belgium came across dozens of bones. They called in a scientist, who identified them as belonging to Iguanodon. After extensive excavations, four Iguanodon herds were discovered. There may have been even more skeletons, but lack of money meant that the project was halted in the 1920s, and a few years later the whole mine flooded.

Many iguanodons lived in the area where the Bernissart mine was later built. They lived and moved around in large herds.

Big and small

Most of the Iguanodon skeletons found in the mine were a new species, which scientists named Iguanodon bernissartensis, after the nearby village of Bernissart. These plant-eating dinosaurs grew to about 9m (30ft) long. But two of the Iguanodons were a smaller, slimmer species known as Iguanodon atherfieldensis. A few fossils of this species had already been found in Europe.

Changing shape

The Belgian iguanodons radically changed scientists' views of how this dinosaur looked. Not only were the skeletons almost complete, but they were also jointed, so scientists could see how their bones fitted together. Previously, only a few Iguanodon fragments had been found, and scientists had reconstructed the dinosaur as a stocky animal with a horn on its snout. The new skeletons revealed that Iguanodon was slimmer and longer, and that the horn was really a thumb spike.

🐾 Internet link

For a link to a website where you can read an Iguanodon fact file and see an animated Iguanodon model, go to **www.usborne-quicklinks.com**

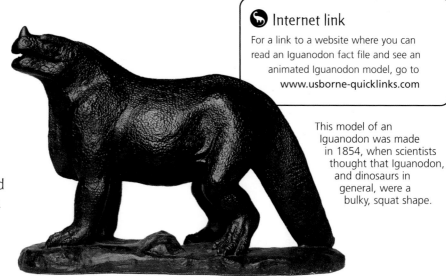

This model of an Iguanodon was made in 1854, when scientists thought that Iguanodon, and dinosaurs in general, were a bulky, squat shape.

Young iguanodons probably stayed with their parents and the rest of the herd until they were fully grown. Adults would have looked after them and made sure they were safe.

A broken tail

Using the Belgian skeletons as a guide, scientists reconstructed Iguanodon in an upright position, with its tail dragging along the ground. But new research has shown that this position is also inaccurate. Scientists now know that Iguanodon stood with its back held horizontally and its tail straight out behind it. It probably moved on four legs most of the time, but could also run on just its muscular back legs.

This early twentieth-century Iguanodon reconstruction looks like a giant kangaroo. Scientists now know that this position is wrong, as the tail could not have bent this way without breaking.

75

This is a stretch of coastline in Dorset, England. Erosion by wind, sea and rain not only creates natural features such as this rocky arch, but also reveals large areas of Jurassic and Cretaceous rocks.

Dinosaurs in England

Many dinosaur fossils have been found in England, particularly in southern areas, where there are large areas of exposed Jurassic and Cretaceous rock. Some dinosaurs from England have been found in other European countries too, as England was joined to mainland Europe in the Mesozoic era.

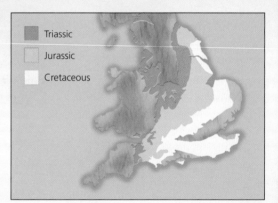

Triassic

Jurassic

Cretaceous

This map shows areas of Mesozoic rock found in England. The band of Cretaceous rock is known as the Wealden and also spreads into mainland Europe.

Mighty Megalosaurus

One of the first dinosaurs found in England was Megalosaurus, a large mid-Jurassic theropod. It was named in 1824, after the discovery of several fossils. These included a lower jaw which was still studded with teeth. Although many later fossil finds were attributed to Megalosaurus, most of these are now known to belong to other dinosaurs. In fact, only a few Megalosaurus bones have ever been found, as well as footprints which show that the dinosaur walked on two legs.

Long teeth are preserved in this Megalosaurus jawbone. At the base of each tooth you can just see a new tooth, which would have replaced the old one as it wore away.

Protected by studs

In 1858, an almost complete dinosaur skeleton was found in early Jurassic rock in Dorset, southwest England. The dinosaur, named Scelidosaurus, was small but heavily-built, with rows of bony studs along its neck, back, sides and tail. Recent studies indicate that it is a primitive ankylosaur. Since the first Scelidosaurus find, another skeleton and other fragments have been uncovered at the same site. All the remains were found in marine rock, which suggests that the dinosaurs were carried by a river into the sea after they died.

Scelidosaurus was not as heavily plated as later ankylosaurs, but its rows of studs and bony neck spikes would still have deterred predators.

Internet link

For a link to a website where you can see a selection of images showing the spinosaur Baryonyx, go to **www.usborne-quicklinks.com**

A giant claw

In 1983, an amateur paleontologist discovered an enormous fossilized claw in a clay pit in Surrey, southeast England. It belonged to an early Cretaceous dinosaur which scientists named Baryonyx, meaning "heavy claw". Later, more bones from the same skeleton were found, including several smaller claws. Baryonyx was a spinosaur, and probably used its giant claw to hook fish out of water. Scientists think that Baryonyx had three claws on each hand, one of which was a giant claw.

The fish-eater Baryonyx probably used its huge, curved thumb claw to spear fish in water. Its muscular arms would have helped it to catch large fish.

Dinosaur island

The Isle of Wight is a small island off the coast of southern England. It was part of mainland England when dinosaurs lived, and was separated by rising sea levels about 10,000 years ago. More dinosaur remains have been found there than anywhere else in Europe.

This is Alum Bay, on the Isle of Wight's west coast. Erosion here reveals late Cretaceous rock.

Fossils everywhere

The Isle of Wight is such a good place for finding fossils because its exposed coastline is constantly eroded by rain, wind and the sea. Thousands of fossils are revealed every year, but many are swept into the sea before paleontologists have a chance to recover them. Many early Cretaceous dinosaurs have been found on the island, most commonly iguanodons and hypsilophodons. The biggest dinosaur so far discovered is a brachiosaur that measures 15m (49ft) from head to tail.

Cowes

Ryde

Yarmouth

Newport

Neovenator

Polacanthus

Iguanodon

Iguanodon

Eotyrannus

Yaverlandia

Hypsilophodon

On this map of the Isle of Wight, the red areas on the eastern and western coasts indicate parts of the island rich in dinosaur remains. Names of some of the dinosaurs found there are also given.

Thousands of skeletons

On the west coast of the Isle of Wight is an enormous fossil bed that may contain as many as 5,000 hypsilophodons. These dinosaurs were small, two-legged ornithopods, common in early Cretaceous Europe. At first, hypsilophodons were reconstructed with one toe pointing backward. This made some scientists think that they lived in trees, using their toes to cling to branches like birds do. However, scientists now know that their toes all faced forward, and that they were fast-running animals.

Hypsilophodons were quick, agile dinosaurs, and healthy adults could probably outrun a large predator such as Neovenator.

Island predator

In 1978, paleontologists on the Isle of Wight discovered the skeleton of a large carnivore which they later named Neovenator. This dinosaur looked similar to Allosaurus and would have been one of the area's main predators, ambushing and killing animals such as iguanodons, hypsilophodons and even large sauropods.

Neovenators were ferocious, fast-moving dinosaurs. They attacked other animals using their large claws and extremely sharp teeth.

New discovery

The most recent dinosaur find on the Isle of Wight is the skeleton of Eotyrannus, which was named in 2001. This dinosaur was a smaller ancestor of Tyrannosaurus. The skeleton is less than half complete, but scientists can tell that it had slim, long limbs and was probably fast-moving. It must have died young, as many of its bones are not fully formed.

★ Eotyrannus had longer arms than Tyrannosaurus, and a smaller skull in relation to its body.

★ Tyrannosaurus was much bigger than Eotyrannus, but it had similar long shin and foot bones.

> ⚫ Internet link
>
> For a link to a website where you can read about the dinosaurs found on the Isle of Wight and discover how they were excavated, go to **www.usborne-quicklinks.com**

79

Asia

The first dinosaur fossils were found in Asia. Chinese documents from AD265 record the presence of "dragon bones", which scientists now think were actually dinosaur remains. A quarter of all known dinosaurs are from Asia, with most of the fossils coming from China and Mongolia.

This map marks two of Asia's most important dinosaur sites, in Liaoning, China, and in Mongolia's Gobi Desert. It also shows some of the major dinosaur finds in the rest of Asia.

Sichuan sauropods

The first sauropods found in China were discovered in Sichuan Province, in 1913. The area is now famous for having more dinosaurs from the mid-Jurassic period than anywhere else in the world. The Sichuan dinosaurs include the stegosaur Huayangosaurus, sauropod Shunosaurus, which had a club on the end of its tail, and sauropod Mamenchisaurus, which had a longer neck than any other dinosaur.

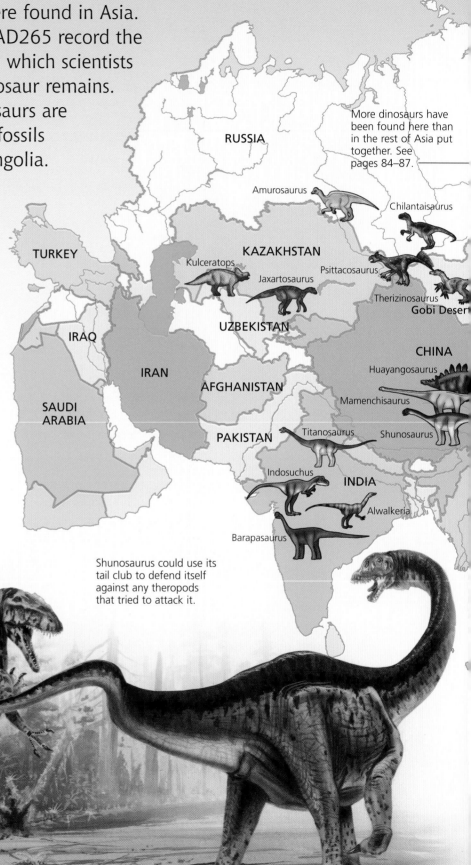

More dinosaurs have been found here than in the rest of Asia put together. See pages 84–87.

RUSSIA

Amurosaurus

Chilantaisaurus

TURKEY

KAZAKHSTAN

Kulceratops

Jaxartosaurus

Psittacosaurus

Therizinosaurus

Gobi Desert

IRAQ

UZBEKISTAN

IRAN

CHINA

Huayangosaurus

AFGHANISTAN

Mamenchisaurus

SAUDI ARABIA

PAKISTAN

Titanosaurus

Shunosaurus

Indosuchus

INDIA

Alwalkeria

Barapasaurus

Shunosaurus could use its tail club to defend itself against any theropods that tried to attack it.

Indian dinosaurs

For most of the Mesozoic era, India formed part of Gondwana and was separate from the rest of Asia. As a result, Indian dinosaurs are more similar to dinosaurs from other Gondwanan continents than to Asian dinosaurs. Theropod dinosaurs called abelisaurs, for example, have been found in India, Africa and South America, but are unknown in the rest of Asia.

Giant claws

The therizinosaurs, known mainly from Asia, are some of the strangest-looking dinosaurs. Therizinosaurs looked a little like giant birds. They grew up to 10m (33ft) long, had feathers on their bodies and toothless beaks at the end of their snouts. Therizinosaurus, the largest of the therizinosaurs, also had huge, 70cm (28in) claws on its hands. Scientists think it may have used these giant claws to reach for food.

Therizinosaurus could use its long claws to bring branches within reach of its mouth. It probably clipped off the leaves with its sharp beak.

Alxasaurus

Alectrosaurus

Tsintaosaurus

JAPAN

Fukuiraptor

Liaoning

Pukyongosaurus

Spectacular discoveries of feathered dinosaurs were made here. See pages 82–83.

Wakinosaurus

Tangvayosaurus

LAOS

Isanosaurus

THAILAND

MALAYSIA

Feathered dinosaurs

In the 1990s, a series of discoveries in Liaoning, northern China, changed the way people think about dinosaurs. Scientists found fossils of small theropod dinosaurs with feathers. These are the fossils that prove birds are directly descended from dinosaurs.

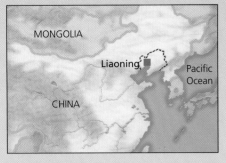

Liaoning Province, in China, is marked on this map by a dotted black line. The red square marks the site where feathered dinosaurs were found.

Buried in ash

The Liaoning fossils date from the early Cretaceous period, when Liaoning was a forested area teeming with life. Nearby volcanoes occasionally sent poisonous gas and ash into the air, killing any animals nearby. The dead animals were sometimes buried in a fine volcanic ash, which preserved the fossils in amazing detail.

The first feathers

Sinosauropteryx was discovered in 1996. It was the first dinosaur fossil with traces of a feathery coat over parts of its body. Scientists think its coat formed a downy layer, which may have helped to keep the dinosaur warm. However, in all other respects, Sinosauropteryx was a typical theropod dinosaur, with sharp teeth, clawed feet and short, sturdy arms.

This is a fossil of Sinosauropteryx. You can see the outline of its feathery coat around its body.

Short arms

Discovered in 1997, Caudipteryx was the third feathered dinosaur found in Liaoning. It was even more bird-like than Sinosauropteryx. Its fossil shows short, downy feathers covering most of its body, and longer, stiffer feathers on its tail and arms. However, its arms were too short for it to be able to fly.

Caudipteryxes may have displayed their feathers like this to try to attract mates, as birds do today.

Tree-climbing dinosaur

Microraptor is the latest feathered dinosaur to be found at Liaoning. It had curved, pointed claws, similar to those of tree-climbing animals such as woodpeckers and squirrels. Scientists think it was able to climb trees and that it probably spent much of its time in trees. Like most birds, microraptors had a toe on each of their hind feet that pointed backward. These toe claws helped them to grip onto branches, so they would have found it easy to perch in trees.

Microraptor had extra-long feathers on its arms and legs, making it look as if it had four wings. These probably helped it to glide between branches like this.

🦕 Internet link

For a link to a website where you can find out more about feathered dinosaurs and see short movies showing how they may have used their feathered arms, go to www.usborne-quicklinks.com

Flying dinosaur

The discovery of a dinosaur fossil nicknamed Dave, in 2000, showed that near-bird dinosaurs had many more feathers than scientists first thought. Dave's feathers sprouted from the arms, legs, along the top of the snout and nearly to the tip of the tail. One scientist has even argued that Dave was capable of flapping flight.

Dinosaur quills

The feathered dinosaurs are not the only interesting fossils to come from Liaoning. A fossil of a horned dinosaur, called Psittacosaurus, showed for the first time that some dinosaurs had quills. The quills were long, hair-like structures, growing out of the animal's tail. Scientists think they may have helped psittacosaurs to attract mates.

This is a fossil image of Dave. Dave has more feathers than any other dinosaur fossil found so far. You can clearly see the long feathers covering its body.

Desert discoveries

Mongolia's Gobi Desert has an amazing variety of late Cretaceous fossils. It is also one of the most difficult places to hunt for dinosaurs. It covers an area twice the size of Britain, has no major roads and is subject to sudden and extreme changes in temperature.

These are the Flaming Cliffs, which surround a large valley in the north of the Gobi Desert. They are 5km (3 miles) long and are made of red sandstone.

A rich variety

During the late Cretaceous period, the Gobi Desert was covered in sand dunes, marshland and rivers. It had enough vegetation to support a wide variety of dinosaurs, lizards and early mammals. Many different kinds of theropod dinosaurs have been found there, as well as sauropods, hadrosaurs, pachycephalosaurs and ankylosaurs.

Flaming cliffs

In 1922, an American expedition led by Roy Chapman Andrews set out to search the Gobi Desert for remains of early humans. However, the expedition became lost and stopped at the Flaming Cliffs to find their way. At the edge of one of the cliffs, the expedition photographer stumbled upon a skull of the ceratopsian Protoceratops. The expedition had little time to explore, but they returned to the site a year later, and discovered the first ever dinosaur nest (see pages 94–95).

Sandstorms in the desert would have been dangerous for dinosaurs, especially for babies, like these baby pinacosaurs. They may have tried to find shelter by huddling behind sand dunes.

RUSSIA

MONGOLIA

Tugrig

Nemegt ■ ■ Flaming Cliffs

CHINA   Ukhaa Tolgod

This map of Mongolia shows some of the richest dinosaur fossil sites in the Gobi Desert.

Barred from the desert

Andrews returned to the Flaming Cliffs three more times in search of dinosaurs, but between 1930 and 1990 Americans were banned from Mongolia for political reasons. Meanwhile, Russian, Polish and Mongolian expeditions explored the area and found many more dinosaur fossils. One expedition discovered fossils of five baby pinacosaurs. Scientists think they may have been buried together in a sandstorm.

Fight to the death

A joint Polish–Mongolian expedition to a site called Tugrig discovered two dinosaur skeletons locked together. The arms of the dromaeosaur Velociraptor were gripping the skull of a Protoceratops, which suggests the two dinosaurs were fighting when they died. Because of this, they are known as the "fighting dinosaurs". Scientists think they were killed by a collapsing sand dune.

★ This diagram of a Velociraptor foot shows how it could flick its second toe claw 180°.

🦕 Internet link

For a link to a website where you can see a photograph of the skeletons of the fighting dinosaurs and find out more about them, go to www.usborne-quicklinks.com

Killer claws

Velociraptor was a small but deadly predator. It was a swift runner with incredibly sharp, flexible claws on its second toes. These claws were always held off the ground to keep them sharp and ready for use as deadly slashing weapons. Evidence for this theory comes from the "fighting dinosaur" find, as Velociraptor's second toe claw was found hooked through the Protoceratops' ribcage.

Velociraptor and Protoceratops were evenly matched in a fight. Velociraptor had sharp claws which it could use to slash through Protoceratops' skin, but Protoceratops' sharp beak was capable of inflicting serious harm.

Spectacular sites

Some of the most amazing finds from the Gobi Desert have come from the Nemegt Basin, a 4,840 sq km (1,870 sq miles) valley in the south of the desert. The first expedition to the Nemegt Basin, in 1948, uncovered a huge number of fossils, and fossils are still being found there today.

Tarbosaurus would have had to ambush a Gallimimus in order to stand any chance of catching it, as Gallimimus was such a fast dinosaur.

Useless arms

The largest known theropod from the Nemegt Basin is Tarbosaurus. It was closely related to Tyrannosaurus, and some people think they may even be the same kind of dinosaur. Tarbosaurus had large teeth and jaws, and incredibly small arms for its bulky body. It could run fast over short distances, although its short arms meant that a fall while running could have been fatal, as its arms would have been useless at protecting its head and body.

Ostrich dinosaur

The most common dinosaur from the Nemegt Basin was the ornithomimosaur Gallimimus. Ornithomimosaurs looked similar to ostriches, although they were about twice the size. Gallimimus was probably the fastest dinosaur, capable of reaching speeds of up to 50kph (31mph). It would have relied on speed to get away from predators, although its strong legs would have been capable of powerful kicks.

Terrible hands

In 1965, a pair of 2.4m (8ft) long arms, belonging to a new dinosaur, were found in the Nemegt Basin. Scientists named the dinosaur Deinocheirus, which means "terrible hand". Scientists think Deinocheirus was closely related to ornithomimosaurs as its arms were similar to theirs, although about four times the size. Like them, it probably ate small animals and plants.

🦕 **Internet link**

For a link to a website where you can find out about an expedition to the Gobi Desert, read journal entries and look at photographs, go to www.usborne-quicklinks.com

These are Deinocheirus' hands. At first scientists thought Deinocheirus must have been a terrifying predator, but they now think that the sharp claws were probably used to bring down branches and to strip leaves off trees.

Packed with bones

In 1993, scientists discovered a new site in the Nemegt Basin, called Ukhaa Tolgod. It is only 50 sq km (19 sq miles), but over a hundred dinosaur fossils have been found there. It is also the best site in the world for fossils of Mesozoic mammals. More mammal skulls from the Cretaceous period have been found there than in all the other sites in the world combined.

Mononykus may have used its claws to gouge holes in termite mounds. It could then have used its sharp beak to snap up the termites.

One claw

One of the strangest finds from Ukhaa Tolgod was a small, feathered dinosaur named Mononykus, meaning "one claw". It had extremely short arms and each arm had just one large, stout claw. Mononykus' arms were too short to reach its face, but they were powerfully built. It may have used them to break into ant hills and to get to insects known as termites, which live in mounds.

87

Australasia

Australasia, which includes Australia, New Zealand and the surrounding islands, has few known dinosaurs, and most have been discovered in the last 20 years. The first dinosaur bone from New Zealand was found in 1979. Most of the dinosaur finds in New Zealand have been made by one woman, paleontologist Joan Wiffen.

Most of Australia's dinosaur fossils come from three areas in eastern Australia: southern Victoria, Lightning Ridge, in New South Wales, and central Queensland.

Polar dinosaurs

For most of the Mesozoic era, Australia and New Zealand were connected to Antarctica, forming a vast polar continent. Even though the pole was much warmer in the Mesozoic era than it is today, the dinosaurs that lived there would have had to survive in harsh weather conditions and long periods of winter darkness.

New Zealand

The first dinosaur bone to be found in New Zealand was the toe bone of a large theropod. Since then, more theropods have been found there, as well as sauropods, ornithopods and ankylosaurs. However, most of New Zealand's Mesozoic rock was formed under the sea, so the majority of the fossils are of marine animals, such as plesiosaurs.

So far, no dinosaurs have been found in Papua New Guinea. This is because it was submerged underwater during the Mesozoic era.

PAPUA NEW GUINEA

NORTHERN TERRITORY

Broome

AUSTRALIA

WESTERN AUSTRALIA

SOUTH AUSTRALIA

QUEENSLAND

Elliot

Minmi

Muttaburrasaurus

Qantassaurus

Rhoetosaurus

Kakuru

Lightning Ridge

NEW SOUTH WALES

Fulgurotherium

VICTORIA

Dinosaur Cove

Polar dinosaurs from the Cretaceous period have been found here. See pages 90–91.

The plesiosaur Mauisaurus was found in North Island, New Zealand. It fed on fish and other sea creatures, which it caught in its sharp teeth.

A shortage of bones

Relatively few dinosaurs have been found in Australia compared to other continents. This is because Australia has very few paleontologists looking for fossils. Much of Australia's Mesozoic rock is also very remote and therefore difficult to reach. However, recent finds show that there is great potential for more exciting discoveries to be made.

Queensland

Many of the Australian dinosaur discoveries have come from Cretaceous rock in Queensland. These include the sauropod Rhoetosaurus, a small species of ankylosaur named Minmi and Muttaburrasaurus, a curious-looking ornithopod with a large bump on its snout. Scientists think male muttaburrasaurs may have had bright markings on their snouts.

Male muttaburrasaurs may have used their snouts to attract mates by waving their snouts in front of a female, like this, in order to attract her attention.

Mesozoic marine reptiles have been found all over New Zealand, but dinosaur fossils have so far only been found on the North Island. None of the dinosaurs found so far has been named.

NORTH ISLAND
ankylosaur
hypsilophodontid
NEW ZEALAND
SOUTH ISLAND

Largest find

In the 1980s, enormous sauropod footprints were discovered in Broome, Western Australia. These footprints showed that gigantic dinosaurs once roamed Australia, but until recently scientists did not have the bones to prove it. Then in 1999, a farmer discovered the remains of a sauropod dinosaur in Winston, Queensland. Scientists are still uncovering its bones. They have nicknamed the dinosaur Elliot, after the owners of the property where the fossils were found. Scientists think Elliot will turn out to be Australia's largest dinosaur.

This diagram shows what Elliot's skeleton may have looked like. The bones scientists have found so far are shaded in yellow.

🦕 Internet link

For a link to a website with information about Australia's most important dinosaur fossil sites, go to www.usborne-quicklinks.com

Dinosaur Cove

Dinosaur Cove, on the coast of Victoria, southern Australia, is one of Australia's best dinosaur hunting grounds. Its cliffs are continually being eroded by the sea, exposing wide areas of Mesozoic rock.

This is Dinosaur Cove. The first dinosaur fossil was discovered there in 1980. So far, over 80 dinosaur bones have been found there.

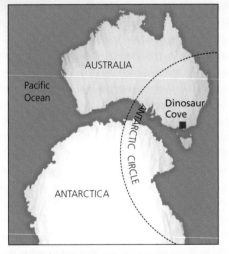

This map shows how close southern Australia was to Antarctica during the early Cretaceous period.

🐾 Internet link

For a link to a website where you can read the story of how Dinosaur Cove was first discovered, go to
www.usborne-quicklinks.com

Cretaceous cove

The dinosaurs from Dinosaur Cove all date from the early Cretaceous period. At this time, Australia had broken away from Antarctica, but its southern tip was still well within the Antarctic Circle. The area would have been light 24 hours a day in summer, but dark during the five winter months. Despite these conditions, plant fossils show the area was forested and fossilized insects have also been found there.

Blasting out bones

Many of the fossils at Dinosaur Cove are buried in incredibly hard layers of sandstone and mudstone. Because the rocks are so hard, paleontologists have had to use explosives to blast out large parts of the cliff face in order to reach the fossils.

Surviving winter

Most of the dinosaurs from Dinosaur Cove were
small ornithopods, such as Leaellynasaura and
Qantassaurus. Scientists are not sure
how they survived the long,
dark winters. Small animals
generally do not migrate far,
as it uses up too much of their
energy, so it seems likely they stayed
in the area. They may have grown plump during
the summer, and in the winter their extra body fat
would have then kept them warm. It would also
have provided them with energy when there
wasn't enough food.

Leaellynasauras lived together in groups.
They had stiffened tails to help them
balance on two legs.

Predators at the pole

Fragments of bone from various
theropod dinosaurs have been
found at Dinosaur Cove.
These include a shin bone,
which scientists think
may belong to an
ornithomimosaur, and
an anklebone, which is thought
to belong to a dinosaur that was
part of the same group of
theropods as Allosaurus.
These predators probably
preyed on the small
ornithopod dinosaurs
during the summer
and migrated away
from Dinosaur Cove
during the winter.

91

Antarctica

Until 1986, no dinosaurs had ever been found in Antarctica. But since then, the fossilized remains of several different species have been discovered, including a theropod that has not been found anywhere else in the world.

Internet link

For a link to a website where you can find out about the different fossils discovered in Antarctica by paleontologist William Hammer, go to www.usborne-quicklinks.com

This map of Antarctica shows the dinosaurs found there so far. Most of the remains were just fragments, so the dinosaurs have not yet been named.

hadrosaur

■ Vega Island

ankylosaur

James Ross Island ■

hypsilophodontid

Queen Maud Land

Enderby Land

EAST ANTARCTICA

ANTARCTICA

SOUTH POLE

Transantarctic Mountains

Ellsworth Land

Cryolophosaurus

Wilkes Land

WEST ANTARCTICA

■ Mount Kilpatrick

prosauropod

Marie Byrd Land

Victoria Land

Cretaceous finds

The fossilized remains of three ankylosaurs and a hypsilophodontid dinosaur, all from the late Cretaceous period, have been found on James Ross Island, in northwest Antarctica. When these dinosaurs lived, it was much warmer in Antarctica than it is today, but there would still have been times of the year when it was very cold. Dinosaurs living in Antarctica may have migrated to warmer areas during the cold seasons.

Ankylosaurs ate low-lying plants, such as ferns. Their spikes helped them to defend themselves.

Bridging the gap

On Vega Island, in northwest Antarctica, paleontologists have found a hadrosaur tooth. Hadrosaurs first appeared around 80 million years ago, by which time Antarctica had already separated from America and Asia. The hadrosaur find indicates that there must have been a land bridge joining South America to Antarctica when hadrosaurs were alive.

Unique theropod

Theropod Cryolophosaurus was discovered in Antarctica in 1991. Bones from three individuals were found 3,660m (12,010ft) up the side of Mount Kilpatrick. Cryolophosaurus was about 7m (23ft) long, walked on two legs and probably looked similar to Allosaurus. It had a 20cm (8in) forward-facing crest on its head. No other theropod found so far had a forward-facing crest.

Male cryolophosaurs may have used their crests to attract mates.

Choked to death

Fossilized prosauropod bones were found alongside the Cryolophosaurus remains. Some of the prosauropod's bones were found in the throat of a Cryolophosaurus. One explanation for this is that the Cryolophosaurus had attacked and killed the prosauropod and was eating it when it died itself. It may even have choked to death on a bone.

This is the camp where paleontologist William Hammer and his team were based during the excavation of Cryolophosaurus.

Difficult terrain

One of the reasons why so few dinosaurs have been found in Antarctica is that 98% of the land there is covered in ice. Although there is some exposed Mesozoic rock, most of it is buried beneath ice up to 5km (3 miles) thick. High winds and an average temperature of -50°C (-58°F) also make expeditions to the region difficult and dangerous.

Egg and nest sites

The first dinosaur eggs ever found belonged to the sauropod Hypselosaurus. They were discovered in France, in 1859. The first dinosaur nests were found much later, in 1923, in the Gobi Desert. Since then, scientists have uncovered many spectacular egg and nest sites around the world.

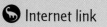 Internet link

For a link to a website where you can find out more about dinosaur eggs and where they have been discovered, go to www.usborne-quicklinks.com

Devil's Coulee, Alberta, Canada

Egg Mountain, Montana, USA

Tremp, Spain

Aix-en-Provence, France

Flaming Cliffs, Gobi Desert, Mongolia

Green Dragon Mountain, China

Tongyong, South Korea

Dohad, India

Kachchh, India

Jabalpur, India

Nanxiong Basin, China

Some of the world's main dinosaur egg sites are marked on this map. All these sites date from the Cretaceous period.

Auca Mahuevo, Argentina

Soriano, Uruguay

Nest design

Some dinosaur eggs have been found just lying on the ground, but scientists believe that most dinosaurs made nests to keep their eggs safe. These nests consisted of a hollow scraped out of the ground or a muddy rim built to keep the eggs in place. Dinosaurs squatted over their nests to lay eggs, perhaps moving around their nests as they laid each one.

Saltasaurs made nests close to each other, though they had to leave enough space to move between them without knocking the eggs.

Egg shape and size

As many as 30 eggs have been found together in some dinosaur nests, often arranged in lines or arcs. Dinosaur eggs are either round or long and thin, and have a rough, wrinkled surface. The biggest egg found is 45cm (18in) long, and was discovered in eastern China. It probably belonged to a therizinosaur.

The Oviraptor eggs on the left form a circle. The mother may have moved them into this neat position after laying them.

This shows the size of a typical dinosaur's egg compared with a hen's egg. Considering the size of most adult dinosaurs, their eggs are very small.

Amazing egg finds

In 1995, scientists visiting a village near Green Dragon Mountain, in China, discovered hundreds of dinosaur eggs embedded in streets and sticking out of cliffs. They even found an egg in the wall of a building, where it had been used instead of a stone. A similar find was made in Tremp, in Spain, where many rocks are so full of egg fragments that scientists named the stone "eggshell sandstone".

Nesting together

Scientists have found large dinosaur nest sites in Montana, USA, and Auca Mahuevo, Argentina. Each site has around 20 nests, built close together. This indicates that some dinosaurs bred in a group, probably as protection against predators. Scientists at the Montana site, known as Egg Mountain, also uncovered older nests underneath. This suggests that dinosaurs returned to the same place year after year to lay eggs.

After laying their eggs, many dinosaurs piled vegetation on top to keep them warm.

Dinosaur babies

Scientists have discovered few remains of baby dinosaurs. This is because the bones of very young dinosaurs were so soft and fragile that they rarely fossilized well. Even those that have been preserved cannot easily be identified.

This model shows an oviraptor baby inside its egg.

Inside the egg

A dinosaur baby developed inside its egg for about three or four weeks before hatching out. Tiny pores in the shell allowed it to breathe, and a yolk provided it with all the nutrients it needed to grow. However, it was quite likely that the baby dinosaur would be eaten by a hungry predator before it had grown enough to hatch out, as eggs were an easy target for dinosaurs and small mammals.

This shows how a baby dinosaur would have begun to hatch.

The baby chipped all the way around the egg to get out.

When hatching, a baby dinosaur used a sharp tooth on its snout to break through the shell. After leaving the egg, the baby had to eat very soon, or it would die.

Preserved in mud

Some of the best-preserved dinosaur babies were found in the 1990s at Auca Mahuevo, in Argentina. The site contained thousands of titanosaur eggs, many of which had babies fossilized inside. When studying these remains, scientists found tiny teeth, skulls and even a piece of skin, which was scaly, like a lizard's. These eggs were so well preserved because they had been buried in mud flows, which prevented them from decaying or being eaten.

This reconstruction of a Maiasaura nest shows babies emerging from their eggs. The babies were about 25cm (10 in) long when they first hatched.

Egg protectors

Until recently, scientists thought that all dinosaurs abandoned their eggs after laying them. This is almost certainly true of large sauropods, which would have risked crushing their eggs underfoot if they stayed nearby. But scientists now know that a few dinosaurs incubated their eggs like birds do. For example, fossilized oviraptors have been found huddled on top of nests in bird-like brooding positions.

This oviraptor from the Gobi Desert was fossilized sitting on its eggs. Its forelimbs can be seen stretched out to the sides, encircling and protecting the eggs.

> 🦕 **Internet link**
>
> For a link to a website where you can read more about the discovery of dinosaur babies at Auca Mahuevo, go to www.usborne-quicklinks.com

Caring parents

A few dinosaurs may have cared for their young. Scientists think this because some dinosaur babies, such as hadrosaurs, had poorly-developed limbs at birth, so they probably relied on adults for food and protection. At Egg Mountain, in Montana, USA, the remains of a hadrosaur group were found. The hadrosaurs ranged from very young to fully-grown, which suggests that parents looked after their offspring. It prompted scientists to name this type of hadrosaur Maiasaura, which means "good mother reptile".

Maiasauras probably protected their young from predators such as small, fierce troodons. Hadrosaur babies took about ten years to reach full size, so they were very vulnerable to attack.

97

Trackways

Fossilized footprints are the most common type of dinosaur fossil. Lots of footprints found together are known as a trackway. Trackways tell us a surprising amount about individual dinosaurs, and enable paleontologists to piece together information about how dinosaurs lived.

Identifying prints

It's rarely possible to say exactly which type of dinosaur made a set of footprints. But different groups have distinctively shaped footprints, so it's usually possible to identify the general group of dinosaurs it belonged to. Here you can see some of the most common shapes.

A hadrosaur footprint

A theropod footprint

A brachiosaur footprint

Tumbler Ridge, Canada

Wyoming, USA

Kayenta Formation, USA

Dinosaur Ridge, USA

Dinosaur State Park, USA

Purgatory River, USA

Dinosaur Valley State Park, USA

La Paz, Bolivia

Sucre, Bolivia

Paraiba, Brazil

Herding together

Many trackways show large groups of the same type of dinosaurs moving together. This suggests that they lived in herds. Very long trackways made by some dinosaurs indicate that they probably migrated long distances as the seasons changed, to search for food or to look for warmer places.

As a migrating herd of sauropods tramped through soft mud, it left behind footprints that later became fossilized.

Worldwide tracks

Trackways can be found all over the world. So far, over 1,000 sites have been discovered, many of which are in North America. The most clearly defined ones formed near where rivers, lakes and oceans were. The ground there was flat, damp and sandy, providing ideal conditions for preserving footprints.

This map shows some of the most important dinosaur trackway sites around the world.

Internet link

For a link to a website where you can find out about Australian dinosaur trackways, go to **www.usborne-quicklinks.com**

Ardley Quarry, England

Münchehugen, Germany

Rioja, Spain
Galinha, Portugal

Demnut, Morocco

Gansu Province, China

Sumchampo, South Korea

Key
- Jurassic
- Cretaceous

Moyeni, Lesotho

Lark Quarry, Australia

Dinosaur attack

Footprints sometimes tell us about particular events in the past. At Lark Quarry, Australia, there are about 3,300 dinosaur footprints made by a mixture of small herbivorous and carnivorous dinosaurs and a large predatory theropod. They suggest that the smaller dinosaurs were attacked by the larger theropod. The smaller dinosaurs seem to have run out in front of the larger one as they made their escape.

These tracks were found in Colorado, USA. They were made by ornithopod dinosaurs in the early Cretaceous period.

Estimating speed

By looking at footprints, paleontologists can tell whether the dinosaur that made them walked on two legs or four. They can also use footprints to estimate how fast the dinosaur was moving when it made the footprints. They do this by comparing the distance between footprints (the dinosaur's stride) with the length of the dinosaur's legs. Leg length is estimated by multiplying the length of the dinosaur's footprint by five.

Sea monsters

While dinosaurs dominated the land, amazing marine reptiles lived in the seas and oceans. They were only very distantly related to dinosaurs, but like dinosaurs, they had all died out by the end of the Cretaceous period.

This is a fossil of Keichousaurus, a pachypleurosaur found in China. It is over 200 million years old.

Land to sea

Around 290 million years ago, some land reptiles began to spend an increasing amount of time in the sea. These reptiles gradually evolved to suit life underwater. However, they never evolved structures that allowed them to breathe underwater, and had to come to the surface for air. Some of the first reptiles to live in the water were the pachypleurosaurs. They had four paddle-like limbs with webbed fingers and toes, which they could use both for walking on land and for swimming in water.

Dolphin-like reptiles

Ichthyosaurs were superbly adapted to life underwater. They had streamlined bodies and large eyes, which probably helped them to see in deep, dark water. Much of what we know about ichthyosaurs comes from amazingly well-preserved fossils from Holzmaden, Germany. Some showed outlines of entire animals, including the fins and flippers. There is even a fossil of an ichthyosaur giving birth.

Ichthyosaurs were strong, fast swimmers. They swam by moving their tails from side to side, as sharks do.

Cryptoclidids were long-necked plesiosaurs. They could move their necks quickly to dart in different directions after fish.

Stone swallowers

Plesiosaurs were a diverse group of meat-eating reptiles. Their fossils have been found all over the world. They all had two pairs of wing-like flippers, and had large lungs, which helped them to stay underwater for long periods of time. Some plesiosaurs, such as Styxosaurus, have been found with stones inside their stomachs. Scientists think that when plesiosaurs had full lungs, their bodies were so full of air that they would have floated to the surface, so they may have swallowed stones to weigh themselves down.

Long necks

Some plesiosaurs had long necks and small heads, with many sharp, pointed teeth. They probably preyed on small fish and other sea creatures. Scientists think they fed by taking in gulps of water and small prey. They then used their tongues to push the water out through their teeth, trapping the prey in their mouths.

Huge heads

One group of plesiosaurs had short necks and huge heads, filled with deadly teeth. These plesiosaurs are known as pliosaurs. They were the dominant underwater predator of their time, feeding on ichthyosaurs, long-necked plesiosaurs and even dinosaurs snatched from the seashore.

Liopleurodon, one of the largest pliosaurs, grew up to 15m (49ft) long. It had large, paddle-shaped flippers, which helped it to move quickly through the water. Its massive jaws and dagger-like teeth made it a deadly predator.

🌀 Internet link

For a link to a website where you can read about Jurassic marine life in Germany, go to www.usborne-quicklinks.com

Flying reptiles

Pterosaurs were winged reptiles. They lived from the late Triassic to the end of the Cretaceous period and ranged from the size of a pigeon to that of a small plane. Pterosaur fossils have been found on every continent, including Antarctica.

Pteranodon

■ Kansas, USA

■ Texas, USA

The squares on this map show the major pterosaur fossil sites around the world. The symbols give examples of the pterosaurs found at each site.

■ Ara
  Plat
  Bra

Wings of skin

Apart from insects, pterosaurs were the first animals that were capable of flapping flight. They had relatively small bodies and hollow bones filled with air, which made them very light. Their wings were made of tough, leathery skin. Some pterosaurs had bony crests on their heads, which may have had bright markings to attract mates.

Triassic pterosaurs

Fossils of Triassic pterosaurs are very rare. One of the most famous Triassic pterosaur sites is near Bergamo, in Italy. Fossils of one of the earliest pterosaurs, Eudimorphodon, have been found there. Eudimorphodon is typical of early pterosaurs. It had a wingspan of less than 1m (3ft), a short neck, sharp teeth and a long tail. Later pterosaurs had short tails.

Eudimorphodon fed on flying insects, which it caught in the air.

Hairy demons

There are many Jurassic pterosaur fossil sites around the world, but two of the best are in Bavaria, Germany, and in the Qaratai Mountains, in Kazakhstan. At these sites, pterosaur fossils have been found with hair-like structures on their necks and bodies. One pterosaur fossil from Kazakhstan was covered in a thick, fur-like coat, which probably kept it warm. It was named Sordes pilosus, meaning "hairy demon".

Like all pterosaurs, Sordes pilosus walked on all fours. Pterosaurs were able to fold their wings close to their bodies, to help them walk.

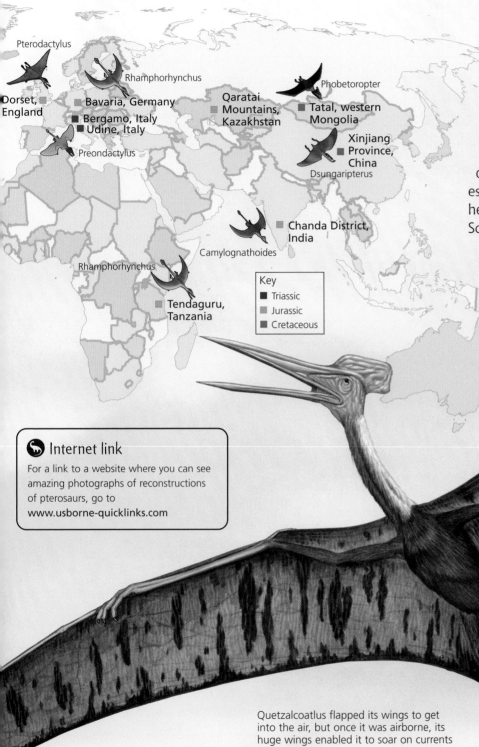

Pterodactylus

Rhamphorhynchus

Phobetoropter

Dorset,
England

Bavaria, Germany

Qaratai
Mountains,
Kazakhstan

Tatal, western
Mongolia

Bergamo, Italy
Udine, Italy

Xinjiang
Province,
China

Preondactylus

Dsungaripterus

Chanda District,
India

Camylognathoides

Rhamphorhynchus

Key
- Triassic
- Jurassic
- Cretaceous

Tendaguru,
Tanzania

Enormous pterosaur

The pterosaurs of the
Cretaceous period were the
largest animals ever to fly.
One of the largest found so far
is Quetzalcoatlus. It was first
discovered in Texas. It had a long
neck and skull and a huge wingspan
of 11m (36ft). Quetzalcoatlus had
especially large feet, which probably
helped it to balance when walking.
Scientists think it may have fed by
wading through shallow water,
picking up fish, snails and
shellfish in its huge beak.

🦕 **Internet link**

For a link to a website where you can see
amazing photographs of reconstructions
of pterosaurs, go to
www.usborne-quicklinks.com

Quetzalcoatlus flapped its wings to get
into the air, but once it was airborne, its
huge wings enabled it to soar on currents
of warm air.

Brazilian bones

Hundreds of pterosaur skeletons and fossilized
fish have been found in northeastern Brazil,
on the slopes of the Araripe Plateau. The site
dates from the early Cretaceous period. At
this time, the area was covered in fish-filled
lagoons where pterosaurs gathered to feed.

★ Pterosaur
Thalassodromeus
hunted for food by
gliding low over the
water with its
lower jaw skimming
the surface, ready
to snap up any fish
swimming just
under the water.

Latest discoveries

New dinosaur fossils are being found all over the world all the time, and each new discovery increases paleontologists' knowledge. Here, you can read about some of the most exciting recent discoveries.

Internet link

For a link to a website where you can find out more about Jobaria, go to
www.usborne-quicklinks.com

This map shows where some of the latest dinosaur discoveries were made.

Thescelosaurus, 1993

Planicoxa, 2001

Sauroposeidon, 2000

Sphaerotholus, 2003

Agustinia, 1998

Tehuelchesaurus, 1999

Dinosaur heart

A nearly complete skeleton of Thescelosaurus was discovered in 1993 with a dark brown mass inside its chest. Some paleontologists believe that this was its heart. If this is true, it is the only dinosaur heart ever found.

This is a photograph of the remains of Thescelosaurus' chest cavity.

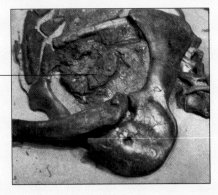

This dark brown circular part may be its heart.

Primitive beast

Jobaria was discovered by paleontologist Paul Sereno in 1997. Although it lived in the late Cretaceous period, it was similar to sauropods that had died out millions of years before. While other sauropods evolved into new species, Jobaria somehow remained the same.

Amazingly, 95% of this skeleton of Jobaria was still intact when it was discovered.

Tiny dinosaur

Scipionyx, a tiny baby theropod discovered in Italy in 1998, is the best-preserved dinosaur fossil found so far. Most of its bones were in near-perfect condition and, amazingly, traces of its intestines, windpipe, liver and muscles had also been preserved.

The only parts missing from Scipionyx were its back legs and tail.

Ampelosaurus, 2002

Histriasaurus, 2000

Byronosaurus, 2000

Scipionyx, 1998

Protarchaeopteryx, 1998

Losillasaurus, 2001

Lurdusaurus, 1999

Jobaria, 1997

Nqwebasaurus, 2000

Giant discovery

Many scientists think that Sauroposeidon was one of the biggest dinosaurs that ever existed. It was about 18m (59ft) tall and weighed about 60 tonnes (66 tons). It was so big that it probably shook the ground as it walked. Some scientists think that Sauroposeidon isn't a new type of dinosaur at all, but just an unusually large Brachiosaurus.

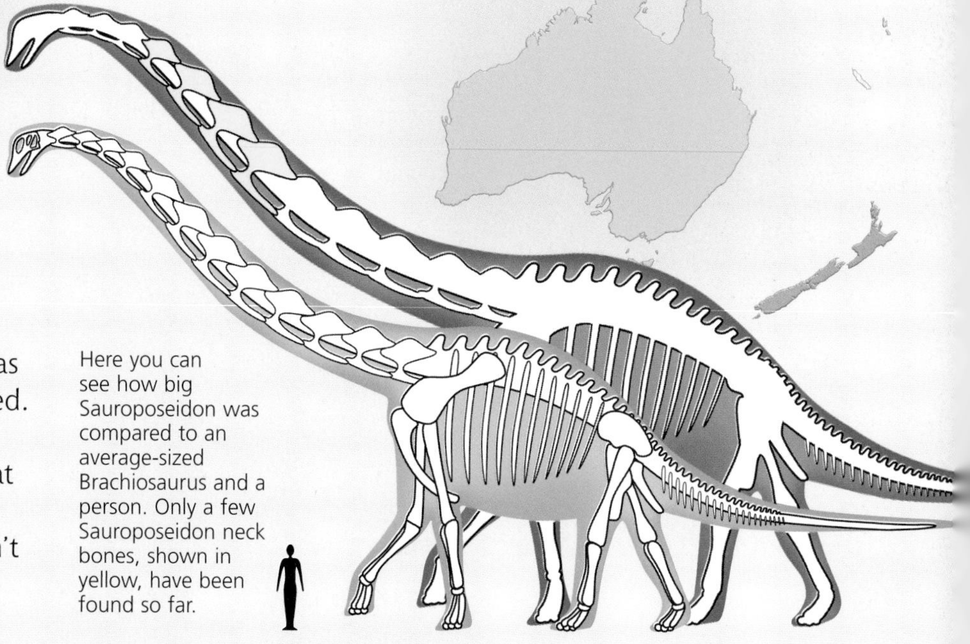

Here you can see how big Sauroposeidon was compared to an average-sized Brachiosaurus and a person. Only a few Sauroposeidon neck bones, shown in yellow, have been found so far.

Sauropods were so large that they could easily overheat in hot sunshine. They probably spent a lot of time in water in order to cool down.

Dinosaur fact file

Here you can find out about famous paleontologists, see amazing dinosaur skeletons and read some incredible facts. There is a quiz to test your knowledge and a fact-packed guide to hundreds of dinosaur species.

Famous dinosaur hunters

Over the years, hundreds of people have been fascinated by collecting dinosaur fossils. Many fossil hunters are professional paleontologists working for museums, but there are also lots of enthusiastic amateurs. Here are some of the most famous fossil finders.

Early experts

One of the earliest dinosaur hunters was an English geologist named William Buckland. In 1815, Buckland identified fossils as belonging to an extinct reptile, later named Megalosaurus. A doctor, Gideon Mantell, also made an early discovery. In 1822, he found fossil teeth in Sussex, England. The teeth resembled those of an iguana, so Mantell named the creature Iguanodon, which means "iguana tooth".

This painting shows the geologist William Buckland, holding a blue bag he always carried for collecting fossils.

Fierce rivals

Fossil-hunting became very popular in the late 1800s. The race to find new dinosaurs led to bitter rivalry between two American paleontologists, Edward Drinker Cope and Othniel Charles Marsh. At first, Cope and Marsh worked together, but later they competed fiercely to find the most fossils. They hired spies to check on each other's progress, and even stole dinosaur bones from each other's sites.

Cope (left) and Marsh (right) named about 130 dinosaurs, including Diplodocus and Stegosaurus.

Intrepid adventurer

Roy Chapman Andrews was an American naturalist who is said to have been a model for the movie character Indiana Jones. He is famous for his fossil-hunting expeditions to the Gobi Desert in the 1920s. These were the biggest and most expensive expeditions of their time. Andrews took dozens of scientists and assistants to help him explore potential sites, and more than 100 camels to carry supplies.

Roy Chapman Andrews found all kinds of fossils on his expeditions to the Gobi Desert, including the first dinosaur nests. Here he is shown holding dinosaur eggs at one of the nest sites.

This is Afrovenator, an early
Cretaceous theropod. It was
discovered by Paul Sereno in
the Sahara Desert, in 1993.

New dino detectives

One of the most famous modern paleontologists
is Paul Sereno, an American who leads
expeditions all over the world. He has found
and named many African dinosaurs, including
Afrovenator and Suchomimus. Another prolific
fossil hunter of recent times is Argentinian
José Bonaparte, whose discoveries in Argentina
include Carnotaurus, a horned theropod.

A fantastic find

Some fossil hunters are lucky enough
to come across really spectacular fossils.
One such person is Sue Hendrickson,
a paleontologist who spotted a few
Tyrannosaurus bones while on a fossil dig
in South Dakota, USA, in 1990. She and
the rest of the team then went on to
uncover the largest, most complete and
best-preserved Tyrannosaurus skeleton ever.

🐾 Internet link

For a link to a website that has
biographies of many famous
dinosaur hunters, go to
www.usborne-quicklinks.com

Dinosaurs on display

Dinosaur fossils are displayed in museums all over the world, often alongside realistic models that show what dinosaurs looked like. Many museums are also involved in ongoing dinosaur research, so they are great places to find up-to-date dinosaur information.

🦕 Internet link

For a link to a website where you can see photographs of dinosaur models and find out how moving dinosaurs are made, go to www.usborne-quicklinks.com

A worker at the Royal Tyrrell Museum in Alberta, Canada, helps move a life-size Tyrannosaurus model into position outside the museum.

Hi-tech entertainment

Many museums use modern technology to help visitors imagine what life was like when dinosaurs lived. One museum in Shanghai, China, screens computer-generated images that recreate sights and sounds of the Mesozoic era. Other museums have robotic models that look, sound and move like real dinosaurs. The models consist of a metal frame and moving parts, covered in a stretchy foam layer that looks like skin.

On the right is a robotic dinosaur from the Natural History Museum, London. The model's head and arms move as it looks around and roars menacingly, and it even has bad breath.

Dinos in New York

The American Museum of Natural History, in New York, has the world's largest collection of dinosaur fossils. The museum is renowned for its dinosaur research, and its many paleontologists go on digs all over the world. Perhaps the most famous paleontologist to work for the museum was Barnum Brown, who discovered many different dinosaurs, including the first Tyrannosaurus.

This Barosaurus skeleton stands in the entrance hall of the American Museum of Natural History. It has been constructed to show how Barosaurus might have reared up to defend itself when attacked.

A huge collection

Dinosaur fossils from all over the world are displayed in London's Natural History Museum. This huge museum has impressive reconstructions of many dinosaurs, including Triceratops, Iguanodon and Hypsilophodon, as well as a 26m (85ft) long Diplodocus in the entrance hall. The museum's paleontologists study new dinosaur theories and collect all kinds of fossil specimens. In 1986, they identified and named the spinosaur Baryonyx.

This Triceratops skeleton is one of the main dinosaur attractions at London's Natural History Museum.

Work in progress

The Zigong Dinosaur Museum, in southeastern China, is built on a site where thousands of Jurassic bones have been found, and where many more are still being uncovered. A large area of rock is exposed in the middle of the museum, so visitors can look down and see paleontologists at work excavating bones.

Timeline

Dinosaurs lived for around 175 million years. They were constantly evolving during this time, with new species appearing and others dying out. This timeline shows when some of the different species of dinosaurs lived.

Pachycephalosaurs and troodontids first appeared in the Cretaceous period. Caudipteryx is the earliest-known oviraptor.

The earliest-known dinosaurs were kangaroo-sized prosauropods.

The letters MYA stand for "Million Years Ago".

Isanosaurus, from the late Triassic period, is the earliest-known sauropod.

Huayangosaurus is one of the earliest-known stegosaurs.

Small ornithopod dinosaurs, such as Heterodontosaurus and Lesothosaurus, first appeared in the early Jurassic period.

Large theropods became more common in the mid-Jurassic period.

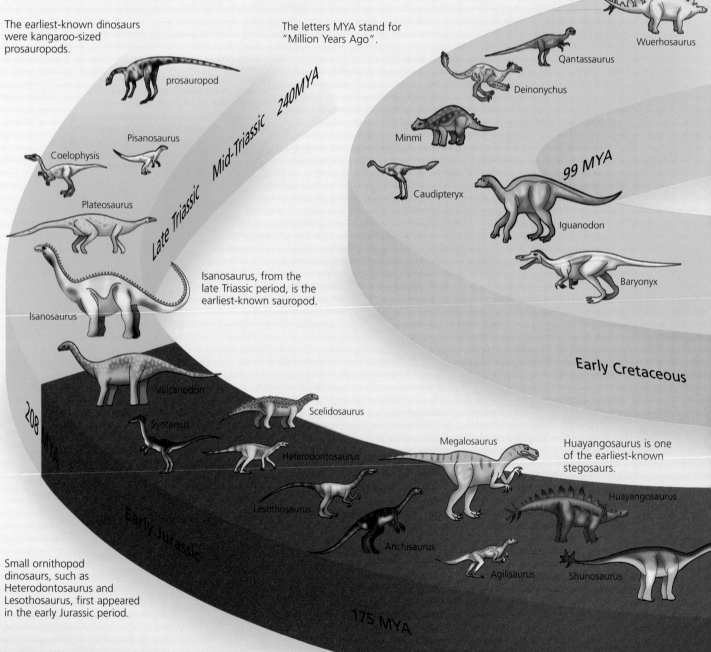

prosauropod

Pisanosaurus

Coelophysis

Plateosaurus

Isanosaurus

Mid-Triassic 240MYA

Late Triassic

Vulcanodon

208 MYA

Syntarsus

Scelidosaurus

Heterodontosaurus

Lesothosaurus

Anchisaurus

Agilisaurus

Early Jurassic

175 MYA

Megalosaurus

Shunosaurus

Huayangosaurus

Mid-Jurassic

Qantassaurus

Deinonychus

Wuerhosaurus

Minmi

Caudipteryx

99 MYA

Iguanodon

Baryonyx

Early Cretaceous

112

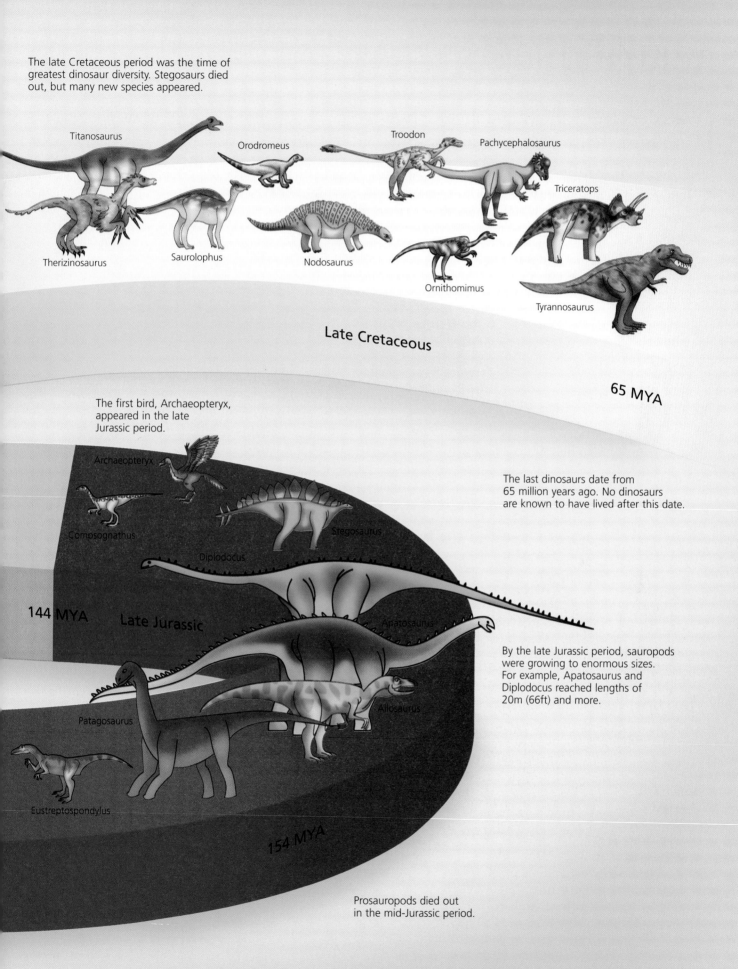

The late Cretaceous period was the time of greatest dinosaur diversity. Stegosaurs died out, but many new species appeared.

Titanosaurus

Orodromeus

Troodon

Pachycephalosaurus

Triceratops

Therizinosaurus

Saurolophus

Nodosaurus

Ornithomimus

Tyrannosaurus

Late Cretaceous

65 MYA

The first bird, Archaeopteryx, appeared in the late Jurassic period.

Archaeopteryx

Compsognathus

Stegosaurus

Diplodocus

The last dinosaurs date from 65 million years ago. No dinosaurs are known to have lived after this date.

144 MYA   Late Jurassic

Apatosaurus

By the late Jurassic period, sauropods were growing to enormous sizes. For example, Apatosaurus and Diplodocus reached lengths of 20m (66ft) and more.

Patagosaurus

Allosaurus

Eustreptospondylus

154 MYA

Prosauropods died out in the mid-Jurassic period.

Amazing facts

Dinosaurs were amazing animals. They included the strongest, heaviest and fiercest land animals ever to have lived. Here are some fascinating facts about them.

Ceratopsian Pentaceratops had the biggest skull of any land animal. Its skull was over 3m (10ft) long, which was half the length of its entire body.

Injuries found on the skulls of large theropod dinosaurs show that they bit each other's faces while fighting.

Tyrannosaurus had the most powerful bite of any dinosaur – around three times more powerful than a lion's bite and nearly 20 times more powerful than a human's.

The sauropod Diplodocus could move its whip-like tail faster than the speed of sound. This would have made an incredibly loud noise, which probably scared off other dinosaurs.

Scientists calculate that an animal heavier than 200 tonnes (220 tons) would be too heavy to move. The biggest dinosaurs probably weighed just a little less than this.

Stegosaur Lexovisaurus had the longest spikes of any dinosaur. Each of its shoulder spikes grew up to 1.2m (4ft) long.

Scientists used to think that only stegosaurs had bony plates sticking up from their backs, but in 1998 a sauropod, Agustinia, was found with back plates. Some of its plates had spikes on them.

The biggest ever land animal is thought to be the sauropod Amphicoelias fragillimus, which was around 60m (195ft) long. However, it is only known from one incomplete backbone.

Tyrannosaurus was one of the largest meat-eating dinosaurs.

Meat-eating dinosaurs didn't grow as large as plant-eating dinosaurs, but they still reached enormous sizes. Theropods Carcharodontosaurus and Tyrannosaurus, for example, grew over 12m (39ft) long, while Spinosaurus may have grown up to 15m (49ft) long.

This is the skeleton of spinosaur Suchomimus. You can clearly see its enormous jaws and sharp teeth. Suchomimus was discovered in Niger, Africa, in 1998.

🦕 Suchomimus had amazingly long jaws. Its skull was over 1.2m (4ft) in length, with an extremely long, narrow snout. The jaws were packed with more than 100 deadly, hook-like teeth, which it used to catch fish.

🦕 Hadrosaurs Anatotitan and Edmontosaurus had up to 1,600 teeth, more teeth than any other type of dinosaur. The teeth were tightly packed together to provide a large grinding surface, so the animals could break down even the toughest plant matter.

🦕 Some plant-eating dinosaurs swallowed stones to help them digest their food. These stones are called gastroliths. The gastroliths tumbled around inside the dinosaurs' stomachs, grinding down their food. Gastroliths are usually found mixed up with dinosaur skeletons, or lying close to them.

🦕 One dinosaur, sauropod Seismosaurus, was found with a large stone in its throat area. Scientists think it may have swallowed the stone to use as a gastrolith, and then choked to death on it.

These are gastroliths. Scientists are able to tell if stones are gastroliths as they have smooth surfaces from rubbing against each other inside dinosaurs' stomachs.

🦕 The theropod dinosaur with the most teeth was the ornithomimosaur Pelecanimimus, with around 200 teeth. This is particularly surprising because most ornithomimosaurs were toothless.

🦕 All dinosaurs had powerful back legs and many had long, flexible tails, which meant they were probably very good swimmers. They may have swum between islands, or even between continents that were not too far apart.

🦕 The smallest dinosaur found so far is the feathered dromaeosaur Microraptor. At 30cm (12in) long, it was only about the size of a hen.

🦕 Ankylosaurs had wider bodies than any other type of dinosaur. This is partly because some ankylosaurs, such as Euoplocephalus, had backs that were almost flat.

🦕 Internet link
For a link to a website packed with games, quizzes and more amazing dinosaur facts, go to
www.usborne-quicklinks.com

Dinosaur quiz

How much do you know about dinosaurs? Test your knowledge with these quiz questions. The answers are on page 137.

Picture round

Can you answer these questions about the dinosaur pictures on these pages? Each has clues to help you.

1. The dinosaur that made these footprints walked on three toes and had narrow claws. What kind of dinosaur do you think it was?

a) A theropod
b) A sauropod
c) An ornithopod

2. The dinosaur below had large, sharp and powerful teeth. What kind of dinosaur do you think it was?

a) A hadrosaur
b) An ornithomimosaur
c) A theropod

3. The dinosaur skeleton on the right has an extra-long second toe claw. What kind of dinosaur is it?

a) A tyrannosaur
b) A dromaeosaur
c) An ankylosaur

4. The scene to the right shows neovenators, hypsilophodons and flowers. Which period of the Mesozoic era do you think it's from?

a) Jurassic
b) Cretaceous
c) Triassic

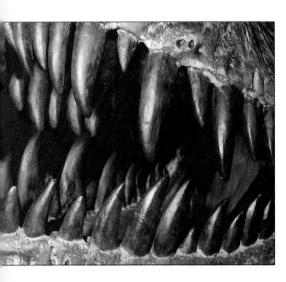

Survival challenge

Could you have survived as a dinosaur?
Take this test to find out.

1. You are a hadrosaur living in North America during the late Cretaceous period. You have come to a turning and must either go left, where a herd of ceratopsians awaits you, or turn right, where a lone Albertosaurus is standing. Which way do you turn?

a) Left.   b) Right.

2. You are a Gallimimus living in the Gobi Desert 70 million years ago. You see a Tarbosaurus in the distance, slowly coming your way. What should you do?

a) Run away.   b) Hide.

3. You are a Leaellynasaura living in southern Australia during the Cretaceous period. Winter is coming and the weather is getting colder. Should you make a long journey to find a warmer area for the winter or stay in southern Australia?

a) Make a long journey.   b) Stay where you are.

4. You are the sauropod Diplodocus, one of the longest and largest dinosaurs. You have wandered away from your herd in search of food when you see an Allosaurus approaching. What should you do?

a) Rejoin the safety of the herd.
b) Stay put. Your size will protect you.

Quick quiz

1. Were the largest dinosaurs carnivores or herbivores?

2. Which continent had no record of dinosaur fossils until the 1980s?

3. Where have the only Triceratops fossils been found?

4. Name the smallest dinosaur found so far.

5. What is the name given to people who study dinosaur fossils?

6. In which country have the most feathered dinosaurs been found?

7. What kinds of dinosaurs had hollow crests on their heads, which they may have blown through to make loud noises?

8. When did the last dinosaurs become extinct?

Dinosaur guide

This dinosaur guide contains facts about most of the different species of dinosaurs. You can find out what each dinosaur's name means and which groups each dinosaur belongs to. The major group is listed first, and the smallest group, which contains dinosaurs with the most similar features, comes last.

ABELISAURUS ("Abel's lizard")
Group: saurischians, theropods, neoceratosaurs
Period: Late Cretaceous
Size and weight: 9m (30ft) long, 1.5 tonnes (1.7 tons)
Location: Argentina
Description: Primitive predator that walked on two legs. It had a blunt snout and is only known from a single skull.

ABRICTOSAURUS ("awake lizard")
Group: ornithischians, heterodontosaurids
Period: Early Jurassic
Size and weight: 1m (3ft) long, 5kg (11lb)
Location: South Africa
Description: Small omnivore with small hands and a short skull. It could walk on two or four legs.

ABROSAURUS ("abrupt lizard")
Group: saurischians, sauropodomorphs, sauropods
Period: Middle Jurassic
Size and weight: 18m (59ft) long, 8.5 tonnes (9.4 tons)
Location: China
Description: Large, long-necked herbivore that walked on four legs. It had a box-shaped skull and huge nostril openings.

ACHELOUSAURUS ("Achelous lizard")
Group: ornithischians, marginocephalians, ceratopsians
Period: Late Cretaceous
Size and weight: 6m (20ft) long, 1.5 tonnes (1.7 tons)
Location: USA
Description: Herbivore with a neck frill with two spikes on it. It had bumps on its nose and above its eyes. It walked on four legs.

ACHILLOBATOR ("tendon hero")
Group: saurischians, theropods, coelurosaurs
Period: Late Cretaceous
Size and weight: 7m (23ft) long, 450kg (990lb)
Location: Mongolia
Description: Large predator with a raised second toe on each foot. It was related to Velociraptor and it walked on two legs.

ACROCANTHOSAURUS ("top-spined lizard")
Group: saurischians, theropods, allosaurs
Period: Early Cretaceous
Size and weight: 8m (26ft) long, 3 tonnes (3.3 tons)
Location: USA
Description: Huge predator with a muscly ridge running along its neck and back.

ADASAURUS ("Ada lizard")
Group: saurischians, theropods, coelurosaurs
Period: Late Cretaceous
Size and weight: 1m (3ft) long, 15kg (33lb)
Location: Mongolia
Description: Small bird-like predator with a small, raised claw on each second toe.

AEGYPTOSAURUS ("Egyptian lizard")
Group: saurischians, sauropodomorphs, sauropods
Period: Late Cretaceous
Size and weight: 15m (49ft) long, 7 tonnes (7.7 tons)
Location: Egypt
Description: Long-necked herbivore that probably had plated skin. It walked on four legs. Its only known remains were destroyed during World War II.

AEOLOSAURUS ("wind lizard")
Group: saurischians, sauropodomorphs, sauropods
Period: Late Cretaceous
Size and weight: 15m (49ft) long, 7 tonnes (7.7 tons)
Location: Argentina
Description: Long-necked herbivore that probably had plates along its back. It walked on four legs.

AFROVENATOR ("African hunter")
Group: saurischians, theropods, spinosaurs
Period: Early Cretaceous
Size and weight: 8m (26ft) long, 820kg (1,810lb)
Location: northern Africa
Description: Predator with a long skull and jagged teeth. It had short arms with three fingers on each hand, and it walked on two legs.

AGILISAURUS ("agile lizard")
Group: ornithischians, ornithopods, hypsilophodontids
Period: Middle Jurassic
Size and weight: 1.5m (5ft) long, 6kg (13lb)
Location: China
Description: Small herbivore with a narrow beak, short arms and five fingers on each hand. It walked on two legs.

AGNOSPHITYS ("unknown ancestor")
Group: saurischians, and possibly herrerasaurids
Period: Late Triassic
Size and weight: 1.5m (5ft) long, 6kg (13lb)
Location: England
Description: Primitive predator that was probably similar to Herrerasaurus, but smaller. It walked on two legs.

AGUSTINIA ("for Agustin")
Group: saurischians, sauropodomorphs, sauropods
Period: Early Cretaceous
Size and weight: 20m (66ft) long, 22 tonnes (24 tons)
Location: Argentina
Description: Long-necked herbivore with spikes and plates on its back. It walked on four legs.

ALAMOSAURUS ("Ojo Alamo lizard")
Group: saurischians, sauropodomorphs, sauropods
Period: Late Cretaceous
Size and weight: 20m (66ft) long, 12 tonnes (13 tons)
Location: USA
Description: Long-necked herbivore with a long, flexible tail, and teeth shaped like pencils. It walked on four legs.

ALBERTOSAURUS ("Alberta lizard")
Group: saurischians, theropods, coelurosaurs
Period: Late Cretaceous
Size and weight: 10m (33ft) long, 2.4 tonnes (2.6 tons)
Location: USA and Canada
Description: Predator with short arms and two fingers on each hand. It had a broad skull and it walked on two legs.

ALECTROSAURUS ("mateless lizard")
Group: saurischians, theropods, coelurosaurs
Period: Late Cretaceous
Size and weight: 5m (16ft) long, 500kg (1,100lb)
Location: China and Mongolia
Description: Predator with short arms and long hind legs. It had a large skull and it walked on two legs.

ALETOPELTA ("wandering shield")
Group: ornithischians, thyreophorans, ankylosaurs
Period: Late Cretaceous
Size and weight: 6m (20ft) long, 2 tonnes (2.2 tons)
Location: USA
Description: Plated herbivore with short legs and a broad body. It had a large spike in the middle of its back and it walked on four legs.

ALIORAMUS ("other branch")
Group: saurischians, theropods, coelurosaurs
Period: Late Cretaceous
Size and weight: 6m (20ft) long, 700kg (1,545lb)
Location: Mongolia
Description: Tyrannosaur with a long skull and a row of bumps along the top of its snout.

ALIWALIA ("for Aliwal")
Group: saurischians, and possibly herrerasaurids
Period: Late Triassic
Size and weight: 8m (26ft) long, 1.2 tonnes (1.3 tons)
Location: southern Africa
Description: Large, primitive predator that might have been similar to Herrerasaurus. It walked on two legs.

ALLOSAURUS ("strange lizard")
Group: saurischians, theropods, allosaurs
Period: Late Jurassic
Size and weight: 8m (26ft) long, 1 tonne (1.1 tons)
Location: USA, eastern Africa and Portugal
Description: Predator with three fingers on each hand and horns above its eyes. It walked on two legs.

ALOCODON ("furrow tooth")
Group: ornithischians, and possibly thyreophorans
Period: Late Jurassic
Size and weight: 1m (3ft) long, 9kg (20lb)
Location: Portugal
Description: Small dinosaur known only from its teeth. It might have been a plated herbivore, and might have walked on four legs.

ALTIRHINUS ("high nose")
Group: ornithischians, ornithopods, iguanodonts
Period: Early Cretaceous
Size and weight: 8m (26ft) long, 3.1 tonnes (3.4 tons)
Location: Mongolia
Description: Herbivore with a huge nose, a beak and spike-shaped thumbs. It could walk on two or four legs.

ALVAREZSAURUS ("Alvarez's lizard")
Group: saurischians, theropods, coelurosaurs
Period: Late Cretaceous
Size and weight: 2m (7ft) long, 6kg (13lb)
Location: Argentina
Description: Feathered predator with a skull shaped like a bird's skull. It walked on two legs.

ALWALKERIA ("for Alick Walker")
Group: saurischians, and possibly herrerasaurids
Period: Late Triassic
Size and weight: 1m (3ft) long, 5kg (11lb)
Location: India
Description: Small predator with sharp, curved teeth that might have been similar to Herrerasaurus. It walked on two legs.

ALXASAURUS ("Alxa lizard")
Group: saurischians, theropods, coelurosaurs
Period: Late Cretaceous
Size and weight: 4m (13ft) long, 120kg (265lb)
Location: China
Description: Dinosaur with a short tail, wide hips and three fingers on each hand. It was either a herbivore or an omnivore and it walked on two legs.

AMARGASAURUS ("Amarga lizard")
Group: saurischians, sauropodomorphs, sauropods
Period: Early Cretaceous
Size and weight: 10m (33ft) long, 6.8 tonnes (7.5 tons)
Location: Argentina
Description: Herbivore with a long neck that had spikes along the top. It walked on four legs.

AMMOSAURUS ("sandstone lizard")
Group: saurischians, sauropodomorphs, prosauropods
Period: Early Jurassic
Size and weight: 4m (13ft) long, 120kg (250lb)
Location: USA
Description: Long-necked dinosaur with five fingers on each hand and large thumb claws. It could walk on

two or four legs and was either a herbivore or an omnivore.

AMPELOSAURUS ("vineyard lizard")
Group: saurischians, sauropodomorphs, sauropods
Period: Late Cretaceous
Size and weight: 15m (49ft) long, 7 tonnes (7.7 tons)
Location: France
Description: Long-necked herbivore with plates on its back and sides. It walked on four legs.

AMTOSAURUS ("Amtgay lizard")
Group: ornithischians, thyreophorans, ankylosaurs
Period: Late Cretaceous
Size and weight: 5m (16ft) long, 700kg (1,545lb)
Location: Mongolia
Description: Plated herbivore known only from a partial skull. It walked on four legs.

AMUROSAURUS ("Amur lizard")
Group: ornithischians, ornithopods, iguanodonts
Period: Late Cretaceous
Size and weight: 8m (26ft) long, 3 tonnes (3.3 tons)
Location: Russia
Description: Herbivore with a bony crest on its head. It could walk on two or four legs and might have looked similar to Corythosaurus.

AMYGDALODON ("almond tooth")
Group: saurischians, sauropodomorphs, sauropods
Period: Middle Jurassic
Size and weight: 18m (59ft) long, 10 tonnes (11 tons)
Location: Argentina
Description: Long-necked herbivore that walked on four legs. It had a sturdy body and legs, and might have been similar to Cetiosaurus.

ANABISETIA ("for Ana Biset")
Group: ornithischians, ornithopods, iguanodonts
Period: Late Cretaceous
Size and weight: 1.5m (5ft) long, 12kg (26lb)
Location: Argentina
Description: Small herbivore with a beak, slim arms and small hands. It walked on two legs.

ANASAZISAURUS ("Anasazi lizard")
Group: ornithischians, ornithopods, iguanodonts
Period: Late Cretaceous
Size and weight: 6.5m (21ft) long, 1.9 tonnes (2.1 tons)
Location: USA
Description: Herbivore with a beak shaped like a duck's beak, and a bump on its nose. It could walk on two or four legs.

ANATOTITAN ("giant duck")
Group: ornithischians, ornithopods, iguanodonts
Period: Late Cretaceous
Size and weight: 12m (39ft) long, 7.6 tonnes (8.4 tons)
Location: USA
Description: Herbivore with a long skull and grinding teeth. It had a beak shaped like a duck's beak, and it could walk on two or four legs.

ANCHICERATOPS ("near horned face")
Group: ornithischians, marginocephalians, ceratopsians
Period: Late Cretaceous
Size and weight: 6m (20ft) long, 1.4 tonnes (1.5 tons)
Location: Canada
Description: Herbivore with three horns and a long neck frill. It had a prominent beak and an unusually short tail. It walked on four legs.

ANCHISAURUS ("near lizard")
Group: saurischians, sauropodomorphs, prosauropods
Period: Early Jurassic
Size and weight: 3m (10ft) long, 85kg (185lb)
Location: USA and Canada
Description: Long-necked omnivore that had a small, pointed skull and a long body. It could walk on two or four legs.

ANDESAURUS ("Andes lizard")
Group: saurischians, sauropodomorphs, sauropods
Period: Early Cretaceous
Size and weight: 18m (59ft) long, 9 tonnes (10 tons)
Location: Argentina

Description: Long-necked herbivore with a flexible tail and broad body. It walked on four legs.

ANIMANTARX ("living fortress")
Group: ornithischians, thyreophorans, ankylosaurs
Period: Early Cretaceous
Size and weight: 10m (33ft) long, 2.7 tonnes (3 tons)
Location: USA
Description: Plated herbivore with a long, narrow skull and short horns. It walked on four legs.

ANKYLOSAURUS ("fused lizard")
Group: ornithischians, thyreophorans, ankylosaurs
Period: Late Cretaceous
Size and weight: 7m (23ft) long, 1.7 tonnes (1.9 tons)
Location: USA
Description: Plated herbivore that walked on four legs. It had short legs and a large tail club.

ANSERIMIMUS ("goose mimic")
Group: saurischians, theropods, coelurosaurs
Period: Late Cretaceous
Size and weight: 3m (10ft) long, 100kg (220lb)
Location: Mongolia
Description: Fast-running omnivore with long, slim arms. It had a toothless beak and walked on two legs.

ANTARCTOSAURUS ("southern lizard")
Group: saurischians, sauropodomorphs, sauropods
Period: Late Cretaceous
Size and weight: 30m (98ft) long, 80 tonnes (88 tons)
Location: Argentina, Brazil and Uruguay
Description: Huge, long-necked herbivore with a wide mouth and slim legs. It walked on four legs.

APATOSAURUS ("deceptive lizard")
Group: saurischians, sauropodomorphs, sauropods
Period: Late Jurassic
Size and weight: 23m (75ft) long, 22 tonnes (24 tons)
Location: USA
Description: Herbivore with a long neck and a whip-like tail. It was large and muscular and walked on four legs.

ARAGOSAURUS ("Aragon lizard")
Group: saurischians, sauropodomorphs, sauropods
Period: Early Cretaceous
Size and weight: 15m (49ft) long, 7 tonnes (7.7 tons)
Location: Spain
Description: Herbivore with a wide body and thick legs. It had a long neck and walked on four legs.

ARALOSAURUS ("Aral lizard")
Group: ornithischians, ornithopods, iguanodonts
Period: Late Cretaceous
Size and weight: 9m (30ft) long, 4.5 tonnes (5 tons)
Location: Kazakhstan
Description: Herbivore with a beak like a duck's beak, and grinding teeth. It could walk on two or four legs.

ARCHAEOCERATOPS ("ancient horned face")
Group: ornithischians, marginocephalians, ceratopsians
Period: Early Cretaceous
Size and weight: 1m (3ft) long, 7kg (15lb)
Location: China
Description: Small herbivore with a narrow beak and a short neck frill. It walked on two legs.

ARCHAEORNITHOIDES ("ancient bird-like")
Group: saurischians, theropods, coelurosaurs
Period: Late Cretaceous
Size and weight: 90cm (35in) long, 1.5kg (3lb)
Location: Mongolia
Description: Tiny predator with cone-shaped teeth. It walked on two legs and is known only from its skull.

ARCHAEORNITHOMIMUS ("ancient bird mimic")
Group: saurischians, theropods, coelurosaurs
Period: Late Cretaceous
Size and weight: 3m (10ft) long, 130kg (290lb)
Location: China
Description: Long-legged omnivore that walked on two legs.

ARGENTINOSAURUS ("Argentine lizard")
Group: saurischians, sauropodomorphs, sauropods

Period: Late Cretaceous
Size and weight: 30m (98ft) long, 90 tonnes (99 tons)
Location: Argentina
Description: Huge herbivore with a long neck and slim legs. It walked on four legs.

ARGYROSAURUS ("silver lizard")
Group: saurischians, sauropodomorphs, sauropods
Period: Late Cretaceous
Size and weight: 20m (66ft) long, 13 tonnes (14 tons)
Location: Argentina
Description: Herbivore with thick, heavy-built legs. It walked on four legs.

ARRHINOCERATOPS ("without-horn face")
Group: ornithischians, marginocephalians, ceratopsians
Period: Late Cretaceous
Size and weight: 6m (20ft) long, 1.5 tonnes (1.7 tons)
Location: Canada
Description: Herbivore with a beak, three horns, a neck frill and a short snout. It walked on four legs.

ARSTANOSAURUS ("Arstan lizard")
Group: ornithischians, ornithopods, iguanodonts
Period: Late Cretaceous
Size and weight: 5m (16ft) long, 1 tonne (1.1 tons)
Location: Kazakhstan
Description: Herbivore with grinding teeth, and a beak shaped like a duck's. It could walk on two or four legs.

ASIACERATOPS ("Asian horned face")
Group: ornithischians, marginocephalians, ceratopsians
Period: Late Cretaceous
Size and weight: 2m (7ft) long, 50kg (110lb)
Location: Uzbekistan
Description: Herbivore with a beak, a neck frill and a narrow snout. It walked on four legs.

ASIATOSAURUS ("Asian lizard")
Group: saurischians, sauropodomorphs, sauropods
Period: Early Cretaceous
Size and weight: 20m (66ft) long, 13 tonnes (14 tons)
Location: Mongolia and China
Description: Long-necked herbivore that walked on four legs. It had spoon-shaped teeth.

ATLASAURUS ("Atlas lizard")
Group: saurischians, sauropodomorphs, sauropods
Period: Middle Jurassic
Size and weight: 17m (56ft) long, 15 tonnes (17 tons)
Location: northern Africa
Description: Long-necked herbivore with long, slim legs and spoon-shaped teeth. It walked on four legs.

ATLASCOPCOSAURUS ("Atlas Copco lizard")
Group: ornithischians, ornithopods, hypsilophodontids
Period: Early Cretaceous
Size and weight: 2m (7ft) long, 15kg (33lb)
Location: Australia
Description: Herbivore with long, slim back legs and a stiff tail. It walked on two legs.

AUCASAURUS ("Auca lizard")
Group: saurischians, theropods, neoceratosaurs
Period: Late Cretaceous
Size and weight: 5.5m (18ft) long, 370kg (815lb)
Location: Argentina
Description: Predator with short arms. It had raised bony areas over the eyes and it walked on two legs.

AUSTROSAURUS ("southern lizard")
Group: saurischians, sauropodomorphs, sauropods
Period: Early Cretaceous
Size and weight: 15m (49ft) long, 7 tonnes (7.7 tons)
Location: Australia
Description: Long-necked herbivore that walked on four legs. It had long, slim legs and a short tail.

AVACERATOPS ("Ava's horned face")
Group: ornithischians, marginocephalians, ceratopsians
Period: Late Cretaceous
Size and weight: 3m (10ft) long, 135kg (300lb)
Location: USA
Description: Herbivore with a beak, a short neck frill and horns above its eyes. It walked on four legs.

AVIMIMUS ("bird mimic")
Group: saurischians, theropods, coelurosaurs
Period: Late Cretaceous
Size and weight: 1.6m (5ft) long, 14kg (31lb)
Location: Mongolia
Description: Long-legged dinosaur that walked on two legs. It had a beak and was either a herbivore or an omnivore.

AZENDOHSAURUS ("Azendoh lizard")
Group: saurischians, sauropodomorphs
Period: Late Triassic
Size and weight: 1.5m (5ft) long, 9kg (20lb)
Location: Morocco
Description: Small omnivore with leaf-shaped teeth. It might have been similar to Saturnalia.

BACTROSAURUS ("club lizard")
Group: ornithischians, ornithopods, iguanodonts
Period: Late Cretaceous
Size and weight: 6m (20ft) long, 1.6 tonnes (1.8 tons)
Location: China
Description: Herbivore with a ridge on its back. It could walk on two or four legs.

BAGACERATOPS ("small horned face")
Group: ornithischians, marginocephalians, ceratopsians
Period: Late Cretaceous
Size and weight: 1m (3ft) long, 9kg (20lb)
Location: Mongolia
Description: Herbivore with a beak, a short nose horn and a neck frill. It walked on four legs.

BAGARAATAN ("small predator")
Group: saurischians, theropods, coelurosaurs
Period: Late Cretaceous
Size and weight: 3m (10ft) long, 55kg (120lb)
Location: Mongolia
Description: Predator with a stiff tail and powerful jaws. It walked on two legs.

BAHARIASAURUS ("Bahariya lizard")
Group: saurischians, theropods, allosaurs
Period: Late Cretaceous
Size and weight: 9m (30ft) long, 4 tonnes (4.4 tons)
Location: northern Africa
Description: Large predator with a big skull. It probably had three fingers on each hand and it walked on two legs.

BAMBIRAPTOR ("Bambi thief")
Group: saurischians, theropods, coelurosaurs
Period: Late Cretaceous
Size and weight: 1m (3ft) long, 4kg (8.8lb)
Location: USA
Description: Small, bird-like predator that walked on two legs. It had long arms, a raised second toe on each foot and a stiff tail.

BARAPASAURUS ("big leg lizard")
Group: saurischians, sauropodomorphs, sauropods
Period: Early Jurassic
Size and weight: 20m (66ft) long, 15 tonnes (17 tons)
Location: India
Description: Herbivore with a long neck and spoon-shaped teeth. It walked on four legs.

BAROSAURUS ("heavy lizard")
Group: saurischians, sauropodomorphs, sauropods
Period: Late Jurassic
Size and weight: 28m (92ft) long, 12 tonnes (13 tons)
Location: USA
Description: Giant herbivore with pencil-shaped teeth. It had a long tail and neck and walked on four legs.

BARSBOLDIA ("for Barsbold")
Group: ornithischians, ornithopods, iguanodonts
Period: Late Cretaceous
Size and weight: 8m (26ft) long, 3 tonnes (3.3 tons)
Location: Mongolia
Description: Herbivore that could walk on two or four legs. It is known only from its backbone.

BARYONYX ("heavy claw")
Group: saurischians, theropods, spinosaurs
Period: Early Cretaceous
Size and weight: 9m (30ft) long, 1.7 tonnes (1.9 tons)
Location: England, Spain and northern Africa
Description: Predator with a skull that looked like a crocodile's skull. It walked on two legs.

BECKLESPINAX ("Beckles' spinax")
Group: saurischians, theropods, allosaurs
Period: Early Cretaceous
Size and weight: 5m (16ft) long, 280kg (620lb)
Location: England
Description: Large predator that walked on two legs. It had a tall sail across its shoulders.

BEIPIAOSAURUS ("Beipiao lizard")
Group: saurischians, theropods, coelurosaurs
Period: Early Cretaceous
Size and weight: 2.5m (8ft) long, 35kg (77lb)
Location: China
Description: Feathered dinosaur with long arms, a broad belly and short tail. It was either a herbivore or an omnivore and it walked on two legs.

BELLUSAURUS ("fine lizard")
Group: saurischians, sauropodomorphs, sauropods
Period: Middle Jurassic
Size and weight: 5m (16ft) long, 900kg (1,985lb)
Location: China
Description: Herbivore with spoon-shaped teeth and a long neck. It walked on four legs.

BIENOSAURUS ("Bien's lizard")
Group: ornithischians, thyreophorans
Period: Early Jurassic
Size and weight: 1m (3ft) long, 12kg (26lb)
Location: China
Description: Plated herbivore that walked on four legs. It might have looked like Scelidosaurus.

BIHARIOSAURUS ("Bihor lizard")
Group: ornithischians, ornithopods, iguanodonts
Period: Late Jurassic
Size and weight: 3.5m (11ft) long, 370kg (815lb)
Location: eastern Europe
Description: Herbivore with grinding teeth and five fingers on each hand. It could walk on two or four legs.

BLIKANASAURUS ("Blikana lizard")
Group: saurischians, sauropodomorphs, sauropods
Period: Late Triassic
Size and weight: 4m (13ft) long, 150kg (330lb)
Location: South Africa
Description: Long-necked herbivore, known only from a back leg. It walked on four legs.

BOROGOVIA ("for the borogoves")
Group: saurischians, theropods, coelurosaurs
Period: Late Cretaceous
Size and weight: 1m (3ft) long, 5kg (11lb)
Location: Mongolia
Description: Long-legged dinosaur that was either a carnivore or an omnivore. It had raised second toes and it walked on two legs.

BOTHRIOSPONDYLUS ("furrowed vertebrae")
Group: saurischians, sauropodomorphs, sauropods
Period: Late Jurassic
Size and weight: 16m (53ft) long, 20 tonnes (22 tons)
Location: England
Description: Long-necked herbivore with long, thick front legs. It walked on four legs.

BRACHIOSAURUS ("arm lizard")
Group: saurischians, sauropodomorphs, sauropods
Period: Late Jurassic
Size and weight: 25m (82ft) long, 50 tonnes (55 tons)
Location: USA and eastern Africa
Description: Huge herbivore with a long neck and a crest on its head. It walked on four legs.

BRACHYCERATOPS ("short horned face")
Group: ornithischians, marginocephalians, ceratopsians
Period: Late Cretaceous
Size and weight: 1.8m (6ft) long, 45kg (100lb)
Location: USA and Canada
Description: Herbivore with a beak and a long snout. It had a short neck frill and short horns. It walked on four legs.

BRACHYLOPHOSAURUS ("short-crested lizard")
Group: ornithischians, ornithopods, iguanodonts
Period: Late Cretaceous
Size and weight: 7m (23ft) long, 2.3 tonnes (2.5 tons)

Location: Canada
Description: Herbivore with a wide beak and a crest on its head. It could walk on two or four legs.

BREVICERATOPS ("short horned face")
Group: ornithischians, marginocephalians, ceratopsians
Period: Late Cretaceous
Size and weight: 35cm (14in) long, 1kg (2lb)
Location: Mongolia
Description: Small herbivore with a short, narrow frill and a narrow beak. It walked on four legs and was similar to Protoceratops.

BUGENASAURA ("large cheek lizard")
Group: ornithischians, ornithopods, and possibly hypsilophodontids
Period: Late Cretaceous
Size and weight: 3.5m (11ft) long, 60kg (130lb)
Location: USA
Description: Herbivore with a beak, a bulky body and short hands. It probably walked on two legs.

BYRONOSAURUS ("Byron's lizard")
Group: saurischians, theropods, coelurosaurs
Period: Late Cretaceous
Size and weight: 2.5m (8ft) long, 25kg (55lb)
Location: Mongolia
Description: Long-legged dinosaur with a long skull and lots of small teeth. It walked on two legs and was either a carnivore or an omnivore.

CAENAGNATHASIA ("new jaw")
Group: saurischians, theropods, coelurosaurs
Period: Late Cretaceous
Size and weight: 1m (3ft) long, 3kg (6.6lb)
Location: Uzbekistan
Description: Small dinosaur that was either a herbivore or an omnivore. It had no teeth and looked similar to Oviraptor. It walked on two legs.

CALLOVOSAURUS ("Callovian lizard")
Group: ornithischians, ornithopods, iguanodonts
Period: Middle Jurassic
Size and weight: 3.5m (11ft) long, 270kg (595lb)
Location: England
Description: Herbivore that could walk on two or four legs. It is known only from one leg bone.

CAMARASAURUS ("chambered lizard")
Group: saurischians, sauropodomorphs, sauropods
Period: Late Jurassic
Size and weight: 18m (59ft) long, 14 tonnes (15 tons)
Location: USA
Description: Large herbivore with spoon-shaped teeth. It had a long neck and walked on four legs.

CAMELOTIA ("for Camelot")
Group: saurischians, sauropodomorphs, sauropods
Period: Late Triassic
Size and weight: 12m (39ft) long, 6 tonnes (6.6 tons)
Location: England
Description: Large herbivore with a long neck and thick legs. It walked on four legs.

CAMPOSAURUS ("Camp's Lizard")
Group: saurischians, theropods, coelophysoids
Period: Late Triassic
Size and weight: 3m (10ft) long, 20kg (44lb)
Location: USA
Description: Slim predator known only from its ankle bones. It walked on two legs and might have looked like Coelophysis.

CAMPTOSAURUS ("flexible lizard")
Group: ornithischians, ornithopods, iguanodonts
Period: Late Jurassic
Size and weight: 3.5m (11ft) long, 270kg (595lb)
Location: USA
Description: Herbivore with grinding teeth and five fingers on each hand. It could walk on two or four legs.

CARCHARODONTOSAURUS ("shark-toothed lizard")
Group: saurischians, theropods, allosaurs
Period: Late Cretaceous
Size and weight: 12m (39ft) long, 6 tonnes (6.6 tons)
Location: northern Africa
Description: Huge predator with three fingers on each hand, and unusually narrow teeth for a theropod. It walked on two legs.

CARNOTAURUS ("meat-eating bull")
Group: saurischians, theropods, neoceratosaurs
Period: Late Cretaceous
Size and weight: 7.5m (25ft) long, 1 tonne (1.1 tons)
Location: Argentina
Description: Predator with long legs, short arms and horns above its eyes. It walked on two legs.

CASEOSAURUS ("Case's lizard")
Group: saurischians, and possibly herrerasaurids
Period: Late Triassic
Size and weight: 1m (3ft) long, 5kg (11lb)
Location: USA
Description: Small primitive predator that walked on two legs and might have looked like Herrerasaurus.

CAUDIPTERYX ("tail feather")
Group: saurischians, theropods, coelurosaurs
Period: Early Cretaceous
Size and weight: 1.6m (5ft) long, 14kg (31lb)
Location: China
Description: Feathered omnivore with long back legs, a short tail and arms that looked like wings. It walked on two legs.

CEDAROSAURUS ("Cedar lizard")
Group: saurischians, sauropodomorphs, sauropods
Period: Early Cretaceous
Size and weight: 13m (43ft) long, 7 tonnes (7.7 tons)
Location: USA
Description: Herbivore with a long neck and long, thin front legs. It walked on four legs.

CEDARPELTA ("Cedar shield")
Group: ornithischians, thyreophorans, ankylosaurs
Period: Early Cretaceous
Size and weight: 8.5m (28ft) long, 1.7 tonnes (1.9 tons)
Location: USA
Description: Plated herbivore with a narrow snout. It walked on four legs.

CENTROSAURUS ("spur lizard")
Group: ornithischians, marginocephalians, ceratopsians
Period: Late Cretaceous
Size and weight: 5m (16ft) long, 1 tonne (1.1 tons)
Location: Canada
Description: Herbivore with a beak, a short neck frill and a long nose horn. It walked on four legs.

CERATOSAURUS ("horned lizard")
Group: saurischians, theropods, neoceratosaurs
Period: Late Jurassic
Size and weight: 6m (20ft) long, 600kg (1,320lb)
Location: USA, eastern Africa and Portugal
Description: Predator with a nose horn, large teeth and plates along its back. It walked on two legs.

CETIOSAURISCUS ("whale lizard")
Group: saurischians, sauropodomorphs, sauropods
Period: Middle Jurassic
Size and weight: 15m (49ft) long, 8 tonnes (8.8 tons)
Location: England
Description: Long-tailed herbivore that might have looked like Diplodocus. It walked on four legs.

CETIOSAURUS ("whale lizard")
Group: saurischians, sauropodomorphs, sauropods
Period: Middle and Late Jurassic
Size and weight: 15m (49ft) long, 12 tonnes (13 tons)
Location: England and northern Africa
Description: Herbivore with a long neck, short skull and thick legs. It walked on four legs.

CHAOYANGSAURUS ("Chaoyang lizard")
Group: ornithischians, marginocephalians
Period: Late Jurassic
Size and weight: 1.5m (5ft) long, 8kg (18lb)
Location: China
Description: Herbivore with a narrow beak and wide cheeks. It could walk on two or four legs.

CHARONOSAURUS ("Charon's lizard")
Group: ornithischians, ornithopods, iguanodonts
Period: Late Cretaceous
Size and weight: 10m (33ft) long, 5.5 tonnes (6 tons)
Location: China
Description: Herbivore with a beak and a tube-like crest on its head. It could walk on two or four legs.

CHASMOSAURUS ("chasm lizard")
Group: ornithischians, marginocephalians, ceratopsians
Period: Late Cretaceous
Size and weight: 5m (16ft) long, 1.1 tonnes (1.2 tons)
Location: USA and Canada
Description: Herbivore with a neck frill and horns on its nose and eyes. It walked on four legs.

CHASSTERNBERGIA ("for Charles Sternberg")
Group: ornithischians, thyreophorans, ankylosaurs
Period: Late Cretaceous
Size and weight: 7m (23ft) long, 1.5 tonnes (1.6 tons)
Location: USA
Description: Heavily-plated herbivore with large, forward-pointing shoulder spikes. It walked on four legs. It might be the same animal as Edmontonia.

CHIALINGOSAURUS ("Jialing River lizard")
Group: ornithischians, thyreophorans, stegosaurs
Period: Late Jurassic
Size and weight: 3m (10ft) long, 200kg (440lb)
Location: China
Description: Herbivore with plates along its neck, back and tail. It walked on four legs.

CHILANTAISAURUS ("Jilantai lizard")
Group: saurischians, theropods, allosaurs
Period: Early Cretaceous
Size and weight: 8m (26ft) long, 1 tonne (1.1 tons)
Location: China
Description: Large predator that walked on two legs. It had three fingers on each hand and large claws.

CHINDESAURUS ("Chinde lizard")
Group: saurischians, herrerasaurids
Period: Late Triassic
Size and weight: 4m (13ft) long, 220kg (485lb)
Location: USA
Description: Predator with sharp teeth. It walked on two legs and might have looked like Herrerasaurus.

CHIROSTENOTES ("narrow-handed")
Group: saurischians, theropods, coelurosaurs
Period: Late Cretaceous
Size and weight: 2.5m (8ft) long, 35kg (77lb)
Location: USA and Canada
Description: Toothless dinosaur that was either a herbivore or an omnivore. It had a head crest and long fingers. It walked on two legs.

CHUANDONGOCOELURUS ("Chuandong hollow tail")
Group: saurischians, theropods, neoceratosaurs
Period: Middle Jurassic
Size and weight: 2.5m (8ft) long, 10kg (22lb)
Location: China
Description: Small predator that probably had a long body and tail. It walked on two legs.

CHUANJIESAURUS ("Chunajie lizard")
Group: saurischians, sauropodomorphs, sauropods
Period: Middle Jurassic
Size and weight: 15m (49ft) long, 12 tonnes (13 tons)
Location: China
Description: Long-tailed herbivore that might have looked like Cetiosaurus. It walked on four legs.

CHUBUTISAURUS ("Chubut lizard")
Group: saurischians, sauropodomorphs, sauropods
Period: Late Cretaceous
Size and weight: 23m (75ft) long, 16 tonnes (18 tons)
Location: Argentina
Description: Massive herbivore with a long neck and long front legs. It walked on four legs and might have had a ridge along its back.

CHUNGKINGOSAURUS ("Chongqing lizard")
Group: ornithischians, thyreophorans, stegosaurs
Period: Late Jurassic
Size and weight: 4m (13ft) long, 350kg (770lb)
Location: China
Description: Herbivore with plates sticking up from its neck, back and tail, and spikes on the end of its tail.

CITIPATI ("funeral pyre lord")
Group: saurischians, theropods, coelurosaurs
Period: Late Cretaceous
Size and weight: 1.5m (5ft), 5kg (11lb)
Location: Mongolia
Description: Toothless omnivore that walked on two

legs. It had a parrot-like skull, a crest on its head and a short tail.

CLAOSAURUS ("broken lizard")
Group: ornithischians, ornithopods, iguanodonts
Period: Late Cretaceous
Size and weight: 3.5m (11ft) long, 600kg (1,320lb)
Location: USA
Description: Herbivore with a beak shaped like a duck's beak, grinding teeth and slim arms. It could walk on two or four legs.

COELOPHYSIS ("hollow form")
Group: saurischians, theropods, coelophysoids
Period: Late Triassic
Size and weight: 3m (10ft) long, 20kg (44lb)
Location: USA
Description: Predator with a long tail, and teeth suitable for catching small and large prey.

COELURUS ("hollow tail")
Group: saurischians, theropods, coelurosaurs
Period: Late Jurassic
Size and weight: 3m (10ft) long, 25kg (55lb)
Location: USA
Description: Small predator that walked on two legs.

COLORADISAURUS ("Colorados lizard")
Group: saurischians, sauropodomorphs, prosauropods
Period: Late Triassic
Size and weight: 4m (13ft) long, 120kg (265lb)
Location: Argentina
Description: Herbivore that looked like Plateosaurus. It had a long neck and could walk on two or four legs.

COMPSOGNATHUS ("delicate jaw")
Group: saurischians, theropods, coelurosaurs
Period: Late Jurassic
Size and weight: 1m (3ft) long, 3kg (6.6lb)
Location: France and Germany
Description: Tiny predator with long back legs and three fingers on each hand. It walked on two legs.

COMPSOSUCHUS ("delicate crocodile")
Group: saurischians, theropods, neoceratosaurs
Period: Late Cretaceous
Size and weight: 1m (3ft) long, 4kg (8.8lb)
Location: India
Description: Small predator that walked on two legs. It probably had slim limbs and it might have been similar to Noasaurus.

CONCHORAPTOR ("shell thief")
Group: saurischians, theropods, coelurosaurs
Period: Late Cretaceous
Size and weight: 1.5m (5ft) long, 5kg (11lb)
Location: Mongolia
Description: Omnivore with a beak and a head shaped like a parrot's head. It had a short tail and walked on two legs.

CORYTHOSAURUS ("helmet lizard")
Group: ornithischians, ornithopods, iguanodonts
Period: Late Cretaceous
Size and weight: 8m (26ft) long, 3 tonnes (3.3 tons)
Location: Canada
Description: Herbivore with a beak and a large head crest shaped like a half-circle. It could walk on two or four legs.

CRASPEDODON ("bordered tooth")
Group: ornithischians, ornithopods, iguanodonts
Period: Late Cretaceous
Size and weight: 7m (23ft) long, 1 tonne (1.1 tons)
Location: Belgium
Description: Herbivore known only from its teeth, which were similar to those of Iguanodon.

CRICHTONSAURUS ("Crichton's lizard")
Group: ornithischians, thyreophorans, ankylosaurs
Period: Early Cretaceous
Size and weight: 3m (10ft) long, 60kg (130lb)
Location: China
Description: Herbivore with plates on its back. It had small teeth and it walked on four legs.

CRYOLOPHOSAURUS ("frozen crested lizard")
Group: saurischians, theropods, allosaurs
Period: Early Jurassic
Size and weight: 7m (23ft) long, 1 tonne (1.1 tons)
Location: Antarctica
Description: Predator with a fan-shaped head crest and short arms. It walked on two legs.

CRYPTOSAURUS ("hidden lizard")
Group: ornithischians, thyreophorans, ankylosaurs
Period: Late Jurassic
Size and weight: 7m (23ft) long, 1.6 tonnes (1.8 tons)
Location: England
Description: Plated herbivore that walked on two legs. It is known only from one leg bone.

CRYPTOVOLANS ("hidden flyer")
Group: saurischians, theropods, coelurosaurs
Period: Early Cretaceous
Size and weight: 1m (3ft) long, 4kg (8.8lb)
Location: China
Description: Bird-like predator with long feathers on its arms and hands. It walked on two legs.

DACENTRURUS ("pointed tail")
Group: ornithischians, thyreophorans, stegosaurs
Period: Late Jurassic
Size and weight: 6.5m (21ft) long, 2.3 tonnes (2.5 tons)
Location: England, France, Spain and Portugal
Description: Large stegosaur with plates sticking up from its neck and back, and spikes on its tail and shoulders. It was the first stegosaur to be discovered.

DASPLETOSAURUS ("frightful lizard")
Group: saurischians, theropods, coelurosaurs
Period: Late Cretaceous
Size and weight: 9m (30ft) long, 2 tonnes (2.2 tons)
Location: Canada
Description: Predator that walked on two legs. It had short arms, long legs and two fingers on each hand.

DATOUSAURUS ("chieftain lizard")
Group: saurischians, sauropodomorphs, sauropods
Period: Middle Jurassic
Size and weight: 15m (49ft) long, 8 tonnes (8.8 tons)
Location: China
Description: Herbivore with a long neck, a stocky body and spoon-shaped teeth. It walked on four legs.

DEINOCHEIRUS ("terrible hand")
Group: saurischians, theropods, coelurosaurs
Period: Late Cretaceous
Size and weight: 10m (33ft) long, 10 tonnes (11 tons)
Location: Mongolia
Description: Dinosaur known only from its long arms. It had three fingers on each hand and thick, curved claws.

DEINONYCHUS ("terrible claw")
Group: saurischians, theropods, coelurosaurs
Period: Early Cretaceous
Size and weight: 3m (10ft) long, 50kg (110lb)
Location: USA
Description: Bird-like predator with a stiff tail, large claws on its feet and long fingers.

DELTADROMEUS ("delta runner")
Group: saurischians, theropods, coelurosaurs
Period: Late Cretaceous
Size and weight: 8m (26ft) long, 1 tonne (1.1 tons)
Location: northern Africa
Description: Predator with long legs and a stiff tail. It walked on two legs.

DENVERSAURUS ("Denver lizard")
Group: ornithischians, thyreophorans, ankylosaurs
Period: Late Cretaceous
Size and weight: 7m (23ft) long, 1.5 tonnes (1.7 tons)
Location: USA
Description: Heavily-plated herbivore that walked on four legs. It had large, forward-pointing shoulder spikes. It might be the same animal as Edmontonia.

DIANCHUNGOSAURUS ("Central Yunnan lizard")
Group: ornithischians, heterodontosaurids
Period: Early Jurassic
Size and weight: 1m (3ft) long, 5kg (11lb)
Location: China
Description: Small dinosaur that could walk on two or four legs. It was either a herbivore or an omnivore and might have looked like Heterodontosaurus.

DICRAEOSAURUS ("bifurcated lizard")
Group: saurischians, sauropodomorphs, sauropods
Period: Late Jurassic
Size and weight: 13m (43ft) long, 7 tonnes (7.7 tons)
Location: eastern Africa
Description: Herbivore that walked on four legs. It had a shorter neck than most other sauropods.

DILOPHOSAURUS ("double-crested lizard")
Group: saurischians, theropods, coelophysoids
Period: Early Jurassic
Size and weight: 6m (20ft) long, 300kg (660lb)
Location: USA
Description: Slim predator with parallel plate-shaped crests on its head, and large, sharp teeth.

DINHEIROSAURUS ("Dinheiro lizard")
Group: saurischians, sauropodomorphs, sauropods
Period: Late Jurassic
Size and weight: 17m (56ft) long, 8 tonnes (8.8 tons)
Location: Portugal
Description: Herbivore with a long tail. It walked on four legs and might have looked like Diplodocus.

DIPLODOCUS ("double beam")
Group: saurischians, sauropodomorphs, sauropods
Period: Late Jurassic
Size and weight: 25m (82ft) long, 11 tonnes (12 tons)
Location: USA
Description: Huge herbivore with pencil-shaped teeth and a long neck and tail. It walked on four legs.

DRACONYX ("dragon claw")
Group: ornithischians, ornithopods, iguanodonts
Period: Late Jurassic
Size and weight: 3.5m (11ft) long, 270kg (595lb)
Location: Portugal
Description: Herbivore with grinding teeth and five fingers on each hand. It could walk on two or four legs.

DRACOPELTA ("plated dragon")
Group: ornithischians, thyreophorans, ankylosaurs
Period: Late Jurassic
Size and weight: 4m (13ft) long, 300kg (660lb)
Location: Portugal
Description: Herbivore with a broad body, and plates on its back and sides. It walked on four legs.

DRINKER ("for Drinker")
Group: ornithischians, ornithopods, hypsilophodontids
Period: Late Jurassic
Size and weight: 1.5m (5ft) long, 9kg (20lb)
Location: USA
Description: Small dinosaur that was either a herbivore or an omnivore. It had a narrow beak and walked on two legs.

DROMAEOSAURUS ("running lizard")
Group: saurischians, theropods, coelurosaurs
Period: Late Cretaceous
Size and weight: 2m (7ft) long, 20kg (44lb)
Location: USA and Canada
Description: Bird-like predator. It probably had long arms and a stiff tail.

DROMICEIOMIMUS ("emu mimic")
Group: saurischians, theropods, coelurosaurs
Period: Late Cretaceous
Size and weight: 4m (13ft) long, 150kg (330lb)
Location: Canada
Description: Long-legged, toothless dinosaur with huge eyes and long arms. It was either a herbivore or an omnivore, and walked on two legs.

DRYOSAURUS ("tree lizard")
Group: ornithischians, ornithopods, iguanodonts
Period: Late Jurassic
Size and weight: 3m (10ft) long, 100kg (220lb)
Location: USA, France and eastern Africa
Description: Herbivore with short arms, a small head and a toothless beak. It walked on two legs.

DRYPTOSAURUS ("tearing lizard")
Group: saurischians, theropods, coelurosaurs
Period: Late Cretaceous
Size and weight: 6m (20ft) long, 500kg (1,100lb)
Location: USA
Description: Large predator that might have been a primitive tyrannosaur. It walked on two legs.

DYOPLOSAURUS ("double-plated lizard")
Group: ornithischians, thyreophorans, ankylosaurs
Period: Late Cretaceous
Size and weight: 6m (20ft) long, 2.3 tonnes (2.5 tons)
Location: USA and Canada
Description: Large, plated herbivore that had a tail with a clubbed end. It walked on four legs.

DYSLOCOSAURUS ("hard-to-place lizard")
Group: saurischians, sauropodomorphs, sauropods
Period: Late Jurassic or Late Cretaceous
Size and weight: 20m (66ft) long, 13 tonnes (14 tons)
Location: USA
Description: Large, long-necked herbivore that walked on four legs. It was probably similar to Diplodocus.

ECHINODON ("prickly tooth")
Group: ornithischians, heterodontosaurids
Period: Early Cretaceous
Size and weight: 1m (3ft) long, 5kg (11lb)
Location: England and USA
Description: Small herbivore with fang-like teeth at the front of its jaw. It could walk on two or four legs.

EDMARKA ("for Edmark")
Group: saurischians, theropods, spinosaurs
Period: Late Jurassic
Size and weight: 9m (30ft) long, 2 tonnes (2.2 tons)
Location: USA
Description: Predator with short arms and backward-curving teeth. It walked on two legs.

EDMONTONIA ("from Edmonton")
Group: ornithischians, thyreophorans, ankylosaurs
Period: Late Cretaceous
Size and weight: 7m (23ft) long, 1.5 tonnes (1.7 tons)
Location: USA and Canada
Description: Heavily-plated herbivore with large, forward-pointing shoulder spikes.

EDMONTOSAURUS ("Edmonton lizard")
Group: ornithischians, ornithopods, iguanodonts
Period: Late Cretaceous
Size and weight: 9m (30ft) long, 4 tonnes (4.4 tons)
Location: USA and Canada
Description: Herbivore with many grinding teeth and a beak shaped like a duck's beak.

EFRAASIA ("for E. Fraas")
Group: saurischians, sauropodomorphs
Period: Late Triassic
Size and weight: 2.5m (8ft) long, 30kg (66lb)
Location: Germany
Description: Long-necked herbivore that had five fingers on each hand and large thumb claws.

EINIOSAURUS ("buffalo lizard")
Group: ornithischians, marginocephalians, ceratopsians
Period: Late Cretaceous
Size and weight: 6m (20ft) long, 1.5 tonnes (1.7 tons)
Location: USA
Description: Herbivore with a horn on its snout, and a neck frill with two spikes on it.

ELAPHROSAURUS ("nimble lizard")
Group: saurischians, theropods, neoceratosaurs
Period: Late Jurassic
Size and weight: 6m (20ft) long, 220kg (485lb)
Location: eastern Africa and USA
Description: Long-necked predator. It walked on two legs and was probably a fast runner.

EMAUSAURUS ("EMAU lizard")
Group: ornithischians, thyreophorans
Period: Early Jurassic
Size and weight: 2m (7ft) long, 35kg (77lb)
Location: Germany
Description: Small, primitive, plated herbivore that walked on four legs. It had a broad skull and small, leaf-shaped teeth.

ENIGMOSAURUS ("enigma lizard")
Group: saurischians, theropods, coelurosaurs
Period: Late Cretaceous
Size and weight: 6m (20ft) long, 270kg (595lb)
Location: Mongolia
Description: Long-necked omnivore with long hand claws, a broad belly and a short tail. It walked on two legs.

EOBRONTOSAURUS ("dawn thunder lizard")
Group: saurischians, sauropodomorphs, sauropods
Period: Late Jurassic
Size and weight: 20m (66ft) long, 15 tonnes (17 tons)
Location: USA
Description: Herbivore with stout, muscular legs. It walked on four legs and was similar to Apatosaurus.

EOLAMBIA ("dawn lambeosaurine")
Group: ornithischians, ornithopods, iguanodonts
Period: Early Cretaceous
Size and weight: 8m (26ft) long, 3 tonnes (3.3 tons)
Location: USA
Description: Herbivore with grinding teeth and a beak like a duck's beak. It could walk on two or four legs.

EORAPTOR ("dawn thief")
Group: saurischians
Period: Late Triassic
Size and weight: 1m (3ft) long, 10kg (22lb)
Location: Argentina
Description: Small, primitive predator that walked on two legs. It had five fingers on each hand, and both curved and leaf-shaped teeth.

EOTYRANNUS ("early tyrant")
Group: saurischians, theropods, coelurosaurs
Period: Early Cretaceous
Size and weight: 4m (13ft) long, 180kg (400lb)
Location: England
Description: Predator that walked on two legs. It had long arms, long legs and a blunt snout. It was probably a primitive tyrannosaur.

EPACHTHOSAURUS ("heavy lizard")
Group: saurischians, sauropodomorphs, sauropods
Period: Late Cretaceous
Size and weight: 15m (49ft) long, 7 tonnes (7.7 tons)
Location: Argentina
Description: Herbivore that walked on four legs. It had a long neck, wide body and sturdy legs.

EPIDENDROSAURUS ("tree lizard")
Group: saurischians, theropods, coelurosaurs
Period: Early Cretaceous
Size and weight: 20cm (8in) long, 70g (0.2lb)
Location: China
Description: Tiny predator with long arms, and a very long third finger. It walked on two legs.

ERECTOPUS ("erect foot")
Group: saurischians, theropods, and possibly allosaurs
Period: Early Cretaceous
Size and weight: 5m (16ft) long, 200kg (440lb)
Location: France, Portugal and northern Africa
Description: Predator with short arms, and hands with small claws. It walked on two legs.

ERLIANSAURUS ("Erlian lizard")
Group: saurischians, theropods, coelurosaurs
Period: Late Cretaceous
Size and weight: 3m (10ft) long, 150kg (330lb)
Location: China
Description: Dinosaur that was either a herbivore or an omnivore. It walked on two legs, and had broad hips and three fingers on each hand.

ERLIKOSAURUS ("Erlik's lizard")
Group: saurischians, theropods, coelurosaurs
Period: Late Cretaceous
Size and weight: 5m (16ft) long, 180kg (400lb)
Location: Mongolia
Description: Omnivore with a long neck and a short tail. It walked on two legs.

ESHANOSAURUS ("Eshan lizard")
Group: saurischians, theropods, coelurosaurs
Period: Early Jurassic
Size and weight: 1.5m (5ft) long, 8kg (18lb)
Location: China
Description: Long-necked omnivore known only from its jaw. It walked on two legs and was probably similar to Erlikosaurus.

EUCOELOPHYSIS ("true hollow form")
Group: saurischians, theropods, coelophysoids
Period: Late Triassic
Size and weight: 3m (10ft) long, 20kg (44lb)
Location: USA
Description: Slim predator with a long tail. It walked on two legs and was probably similar to Coelophysis.

EUHELOPUS ("true marsh foot")
Group: saurischians, sauropodomorphs, sauropods
Period: Late Jurassic
Size and weight: 10m (33ft) long, 8.5 tonnes (9.4 tons)
Location: China
Description: Herbivore that had a very long neck and long legs. It walked on four legs.

EUOPLOCEPHALUS ("well-protected head")
Group: ornithischians, thyreophorans, ankylosaurs
Period: Late Cretaceous
Size and weight: 6m (20ft) long, 2.3 tonnes (2.5 tons)
Location: USA and Canada
Description: Large, plated herbivore with stocky legs. It had a stiff tail with a club at the end and walked on two legs.

EURONYCHODON ("European claw tooth")
Group: saurischians, theropods, coelurosaurs
Period: Late Cretaceous
Size and weight: 1m (3ft) long, 6kg (13lb)
Location: Portugal and Uzbekistan
Description: Small predator that walked on two legs, known only from its teeth.

EUSKELOSAURUS ("good-legged lizard")
Group: saurischians, sauropodomorphs, prosauropods
Period: Late Triassic
Size and weight: 9m (30ft) long, 3.5 tonnes (3.9 tons)
Location: southern Africa
Description: Herbivore with a bulky body and a long neck and tail. It walked on four legs.

EUSTREPTOSPONDYLUS ("well-curved vertebrae")
Group: saurischians, theropods, spinosaurs
Period: Middle Jurassic
Size and weight: 5m (16ft) long, 220kg (485lb)
Location: England
Description: Predator known only from one skeleton. It walked on two legs and looked like Megalosaurus.

FUKUIRAPTOR ("Fukui thief")
Group: saurischians, theropods, allosaurs
Period: Early Cretaceous
Size and weight: 4m (13ft) long, 180kg (400lb)
Location: Japan
Description: Predator with curved hand claws. It walked on two legs and looked like Allosaurus.

FUKUISAURUS ("Fukui lizard")
Group: ornithischians, ornithopods, iguanodonts
Period: Early Cretaceous
Size and weight: 5m (16ft) long, 1 tonne (1.1 tons)
Location: Japan
Description: Herbivore known only from its teeth and parts of its skull.

FULGUROTHERIUM ("lightning beast")
Group: ornithischians, ornithopods, hypsilophodontids
Period: Early Cretaceous
Size and weight: 1.5m (5ft) long, 9kg (20lb)
Location: Australia
Description: Herbivore with short arms, long hind legs and a short skull. It walked on two legs.

GALLIMIMUS ("chicken mimic")
Group: saurischians, theropods, coelurosaurs
Period: Late Cretaceous
Size and weight: 6m (20ft) long, 580kg (1,280lb)
Location: Mongolia
Description: Fast-running omnivore with a toothless beak and long, slim arms.

GALTONIA ("for Galton")
Group: ornithischians
Period: Late Jurassic
Size and weight: 1m (3ft) long, 4kg (8.8lb)
Location: USA
Description: Dinosaur known only from its leaf-shaped teeth. It was either a herbivore or an omnivore, and probably looked like Lesothosaurus.

GARGOYLEOSAURUS ("gargoyle lizard")
Group: ornithischians, thyreophorans, ankylosaurs
Period: Late Jurassic
Size and weight: 3m (10ft) long, 1.2 tonnes (1.3 tons)
Location: USA
Description: Plated herbivore with a narrow beak and horns on its head. It walked on four legs.

GARUDIMIMUS ("Garuda mimic")
Group: saurischians, theropods, coelurosaurs
Period: Late Cretaceous
Size and weight: 2.5m (8ft) long, 90kg (200lb)
Location: Mongolia
Description: Toothless dinosaur with a horn near its eyes. It was an omnivore and walked on two legs.

GASOSAURUS ("gas lizard")
Group: saurischians, theropods, coelurosaurs
Period: Middle Jurassic
Size and weight: 4m (13ft) long, 70kg (155lb)
Location: China
Description: Predator with sharp teeth and three curved claws on each hand. It walked on two legs. Not much is known about it.

GASPARINISAURA ("Gasparini's lizard")
Group: ornithischians, ornithopods, iguanodonts
Period: Late Cretaceous
Size and weight: 1m (3ft) long, 10kg (22lb)
Location: Argentina
Description: Small herbivore with a narrow beak and long back legs. It walked on two legs.

GASTONIA ("for Gaston")
Group: ornithischians, thyreophorans, ankylosaurs
Period: Early Cretaceous
Size and weight: 6m (20ft) long, 1.3 tonnes (1.4 tons)
Location: USA
Description: Plated herbivore with long, curved spikes on its shoulders. It walked on four legs.

GENUSAURUS ("knee lizard")
Group: saurischians, theropods, neoceratosaurs
Period: Late Cretaceous
Size and weight: 5.5m (18ft) long, 370kg (815lb)
Location: France
Description: Predator known only from leg and hip bones. It walked on two legs and might have been similar to Carnotaurus.

GENYODECTES ("jaw biter")
Group: saurischians, theropods, and possibly neoceratosaurs
Period: Late Cretaceous
Size and weight: 7.5m (25ft) long, 1 tonne (1.1 tons)
Location: Argentina
Description: Large predator with curved teeth. It walked on two legs and is known only from part of its skull.

GERANOSAURUS ("crane lizard")
Group: ornithischians, heterodontosaurids
Period: Early Jurassic
Size and weight: 1m (3ft) long, 5kg (11lb)
Location: South Africa
Description: Small omnivore that could walk on two or four legs.

GIGANOTOSAURUS ("southern lizard")
Group: saurischians, theropods, allosaurs
Period: Late Cretaceous
Size and weight: 12.5m (41ft) long, 6.5 tonnes (7.2 tons)
Location: Argentina
Description: Giant predator with a huge skull, short arms and stocky hind legs. It walked on two legs.

GILMOREOSAURUS ("Gilmore's lizard")
Group: ornithischians, ornithopods, iguanodonts
Period: Late Cretaceous
Size and weight: 4m (13ft) long, 700kg (1,545lb)
Location: China
Description: Herbivore with a beak like a duck's beak, and grinding teeth. It could walk on two or four legs.

GLYPTODONTOPELTA ("Glyptodon shield")
Group: ornithischians, thyreophorans, ankylosaurs
Period: Late Cretaceous
Size and weight: 7m (23ft) long, 1.5 tonnes (1.7 tons)
Location: USA
Description: Short-legged herbivore with tough plates covering its back. It walked on four legs.

GOBISAURUS ("Gobi lizard")
Group: ornithischians, thyreophorans, ankylosaurs
Period: Early Cretaceous
Size and weight: 6m (20ft) long, 1.3 tonnes (1.4 tons)
Location: China
Description: Plated herbivore with a narrow beak and small teeth. It walked on four legs.

GOJIRASAURUS ("Godzilla lizard")
Group: saurischians, theropods, coelophysoids
Period: Late Triassic
Size and weight: 5.5m (18ft) long, 250kg (550lb)
Location: USA
Description: Predator that probably had a long tail and sharp teeth. It walked on two legs.

GONDWANATITAN ("Gondwana titan")
Group: saurischians, sauropodomorphs, sauropods
Period: Late Cretaceous
Size and weight: 7m (23ft) long, 2.5 tonnes (2.8 tons)
Location: Brazil
Description: Large, long-necked herbivore with long, slim legs and a broad body. It walked on four legs.

GONGBUSAURUS ("Kung Pu lizard")
Group: ornithischians, ornithopods, and possibly hypsilophodontids
Period: Late Jurassic
Size and weight: 1.5m (5ft) long, 9kg (20lb)
Location: China
Description: Herbivore that might have been similar to Hypsilophodon. It walked on two legs.

GONGXIANOSAURUS ("Gonxian lizard")
Group: saurischians, sauropodomorphs, and possibly prosauropods
Period: Early Jurassic
Size and weight: 14m (46ft) long, 7 tonnes (7.7 tons)
Location: China
Description: Long-necked herbivore with a blunt snout and a long tail. It walked on four legs.

GORGOSAURUS ("fierce lizard")
Group: saurischians, theropods, coelurosaurs
Period: Late Cretaceous
Size and weight: 8m (26ft) long, 2.5 tonnes (2.8 tons)
Location: USA and Canada
Description: Long-legged predator with short arms and two fingers on each hand. It walked on two legs.

GOYOCEPHALE ("adorned head")
Group: ornithischians, marginocephalians, pachycephalosaurs
Period: Late Cretaceous
Size and weight: 3m (10ft) long, 100kg (220lb)
Location: Mongolia
Description: Herbivore with a beak, a wide body and short arms. It walked on two legs.

GRACILICERATOPS ("slender horned face")
Group: ornithischians, marginocephalians, ceratopsians
Period: Late Cretaceous
Size and weight: 90cm (35in), 5kg (11lb)
Location: Mongolia
Description: Small herbivore with a narrow beak and a short neck frill. It walked on two legs.

GRAVITHOLUS ("heavy dome")
Group: ornithischians, marginocephalians, pachycephalosaurs
Period: Late Cretaceous
Size and weight: 3m (10ft) long, 100kg (220lb)
Location: Canada
Description: Herbivore known only from the top of its skull. It walked on two legs and had a beak.

GRYPOSAURUS ("hook-nosed lizard")
Group: ornithischians, ornithopods, iguanodonts
Period: Late Cretaceous
Size and weight: 8m (26ft) long, 3 tonnes (3.3 tons)
Location: Canada
Description: Herbivore with a beak shaped like a duck's beak, and an arched crest on its nose. It could walk on two or four legs.

GUAIBASAURUS ("Guaiba lizard")
Group: saurischians, and possibly theropods
Period: Late Triassic
Size and weight: 2m (7ft) long, 20kg (44lb)
Location: Brazil
Description: Primitive predator known only from leg and hip bones. It walked on two legs.

HADROSAURUS ("bulky lizard")
Group: ornithischians, ornithopods, iguanodonts
Period: Late Cretaceous
Size and weight: 7m (23ft) long, 2.3 tonnes (2.5 tons)
Location: USA
Description: Herbivore with a beak shaped like a duck's beak, and grinding teeth. It could walk on two or four legs.

HALTICOSAURUS ("Nimble lizard")
Group: saurischians, theropods, coelophysoids
Period: Late Triassic

Size and weight: 5.5m (18ft), 250kg (550lb)
Location: Germany
Description: Slim predator that walked on two legs. It had four fingers on each hand, a long tail and a long skull.

HAPLOCANTHOSAURUS ("simple-spined lizard")
Group: saurischians, sauropodomorphs, sauropods
Period: Late Jurassic
Size and weight: 20m (66ft) long, 15 tonnes (17 tons)
Location: USA
Description: Herbivore with a long neck and tail, and sturdy legs. It walked on four legs.

HARPYMIMUS ("Harpy mimic")
Group: saurischians, theropods, coelurosaurs
Period: Late Cretaceous
Size and weight: 3m (10ft) long, 125kg (275lb)
Location: Mongolia
Description: Long-legged omnivore that walked on two legs. It had small, cone-shaped teeth.

HERRERASAURUS ("Herrera's lizard")
Group: saurischians, herrerasaurids
Period: Late Triassic
Size and weight: 4m (13ft) long, 220kg (485lb)
Location: Argentina
Description: Primitive predator with five fingers on each hand. It walked on two legs and had long, sharp teeth.

HESPEROSAURUS ("western lizard")
Group: ornithischians, thyreophorans, stegosaurs
Period: Late Jurassic
Size and weight: 6m (20ft) long, 1.8 tonnes (2 tons)
Location: USA
Description: Herbivore with plates and spikes sticking up from its neck, back and tail. It walked on four legs.

HETERODONTOSAURUS ("different toothed lizard")
Group: ornithischians, heterodontosaurids
Period: Early Jurassic
Size and weight: 1m (3ft) long, 5kg (11lb)
Location: South Africa
Description: Small omnivore with fang-like front teeth. It could walk on two or four legs.

HISTRIASAURUS ("Istria lizard")
Group: saurischians, sauropodomorphs, sauropods
Period: Early Cretaceous
Size and weight: 20m (66ft) long, 14 tonnes (15 tons)
Location: eastern Europe
Description: Herbivore with a long neck and tail, and a ridge along its back. It walked on four legs.

HOMALOCEPHALE ("level head")
Group: ornithischians, marginocephalians, pachycephalosaurs
Period: Late Cretaceous
Size and weight: 3m (10ft) long, 95kg (210lb)
Location: Mongolia
Description: Herbivore with a broad body, short arms and a beak. It had a thick skull, which was flat on the top, and walked on two legs.

HOPLITOSAURUS ("shield lizard")
Group: ornithischians, thyreophorans, ankylosaurs
Period: Early Cretaceous
Size and weight: 5m (16ft) long, 800kg (1,765lb)
Location: USA
Description: Plated herbivore that was similar to Polacanthus. It walked on four legs.

HUABEISAURUS ("North China lizard")
Group: saurischians, sauropodomorphs, sauropods
Period: Late Cretaceous
Size and weight: 15m (49ft) long, 14 tonnes (15 tons)
Location: China
Description: Herbivore with a long, broad neck and a long body. It walked on four legs.

HUAYANGOSAURUS ("Sichuan lizard")
Group: ornithischians, thyreophorans, stegosaurs
Period: Middle Jurassic
Size and weight: 4m (13ft) long, 300kg (660lb)
Location: China
Description: Herbivore with plates and spikes sticking up from its neck, back and tail. It walked on four legs.

HUDEISAURUS ("butterfly lizard")
Group: saurischians, sauropodomorphs, sauropods
Period: Late Jurassic
Size and weight: 30m (98ft) long, 70 tonnes (77 tons)
Location: China
Description: Giant herbivore with a long neck and large thumb claws. It walked on four legs.

HULSANPES ("Khulsan lizard")
Group: saurischians, theropods, coelurosaurs
Period: Late Cretaceous
Size and weight: 1m (3ft) long, 6kg (13lb)
Location: Mongolia
Description: Small, bird-like predator with a small, raised claw on its second toe.

HYLAEOSAURUS ("Wealden lizard")
Group: ornithischians, thyreophorans, ankylosaurs
Period: Early Cretaceous
Size and weight: 4m (13ft) long, 500kg (1,100lb)
Location: England
Description: Plated herbivore with long spikes on its shoulders. It walked on four legs.

HYPACROSAURUS ("nearly highest lizard")
Group: ornithischians, ornithopods, iguanodonts
Period: Late Cretaceous
Size and weight: 9m (30ft) long, 4.3 tonnes (4.7 tons)
Location: Canada
Description: Herbivore with a beak shaped like a duck's beak, and a plate-shaped head crest.

HYPSELOSAURUS ("high lizard")
Group: saurischians, sauropodomorphs, sauropods
Period: Late Cretaceous
Size and weight: 8m (26ft) long, 3 tonnes (3.3 tons)
Location: France and Spain
Description: Long-necked herbivore with a broad body and column-like legs. It walked on four legs.

HYPSILOPHODON ("Hysilophus tooth")
Group: ornithischians, ornithopods, hypsilophodontids
Period: Late Jurassic and Early Cretaceous
Size and weight: 1.4m (4.6ft) long, 7kg (15lb)
Location: England, Germany, Spain, Portugal, Romania and USA
Description: Small herbivore that walked on two legs. It had a narrow beak, large eyes and long claws on its toes.

IGUANODON ("iguana tooth")
Group: ornithischians, ornithopods, iguanodonts
Period: Early Cretaceous
Size and weight: 8m (26ft) long, 3.7 tonnes (4.1 tons)
Location: England, France, Spain, Belgium, Germany, USA and Mongolia
Description: Herbivore with spike-shaped thumbs and grinding teeth. It could walk on two or four legs.

ILOKOLESIA ("flesh-eating reptile")
Group: saurischians, theropods, neoceratosaurs
Period: Late Cretaceous
Size and weight: 6m (20ft) long, 700kg (1,545lb)
Location: Argentina
Description: Predator that walked on two legs. It was related to Abelisaurus and Carnotaurus.

INCISIVOSAURUS ("incisor lizard")
Group: saurischians, theropods, coelurosaurs
Period: Early Cretaceous
Size and weight: 1m (3ft) long, 4kg (8.8lb)
Location: China
Description: Dinosaur that was either a herbivore or an omnivore. It walked on two legs and had a short skull, a beak and buck-teeth.

INDOSAURUS ("Indian lizard")
Group: saurischians, theropods, neoceratosaurs
Period: Late Cretaceous
Size and weight: 6.5m (21ft) long, 750kg (1,655lb)
Location: India
Description: Predator with blunt horns above its eyes. It walked on two legs and might have been similar to Carnotaurus.

INDOSUCHUS ("Indian crocodile")
Group: saurischians, theropods, neoceratosaurs
Period: Late Cretaceous
Size and weight: 7.5m (25ft) long, 1 tonne (1.1 tons)

Location: India
Description: Predator that walked on two legs. It had a snout and might have had bony ridges above its eyes.

INGENIA ("for Ingeni")
Group: saurischians, theropods, coelurosaurs
Period: Late Cretaceous
Size and weight: 1.5m (5ft) long, 5kg (11lb)
Location: Mongolia
Description: Toothless dinosaur with a head shaped like a parrot's head. It walked on two legs and was either a herbivore or an omnivore.

IRRITATOR ("Irritator")
Group: saurischians, theropods, spinosaurs
Period: Early Cretaceous
Size and weight: 6m (20ft) long, 600kg (1,320lb)
Location: Brazil
Description: Predator with a narrow skull like a crocodile's skull. It had a low crest above its eyes and walked on two legs.

ISANOSAURUS ("Isan lizard")
Group: saurischians, sauropodomorphs, sauropods
Period: Late Triassic
Size and weight: 12m (39ft) long, 6 tonnes (6.6 tons)
Location: Thailand
Description: Primitive herbivore that walked on four legs. It had column-like legs and a long neck.

ITEMIRUS ("of Itemir")
Group: saurischians, theropods, coelurosaurs
Period: Late Cretaceous
Size and weight: 4m (13ft) long, 180kg (395lb)
Location: Mongolia
Description: Dinosaur known only from a partial skull. It might have been similar to tyrannosaurs.

JANENSCHIA ("for Janensch")
Group: saurischians, sauropodomorphs, sauropods
Period: Late Jurassic
Size and weight: 18m (59ft) long, 14 tonnes (15 tons)
Location: eastern Africa
Description: Large herbivore with sturdy legs and a long neck. It walked on four legs.

JAXARTOSAURUS ("Jaxartes lizard")
Group: ornithischians, ornithopods, iguanodonts
Period: Late Cretaceous
Size and weight: 9m (30ft) long, 4 tonnes (4.5 tons)
Location: Kazakhstan
Description: Herbivore with a beak shaped like a duck's beak. It probably had a plate-like crest on its skull and it could walk on two or four legs.

JEHOLOSAURUS ("Jehol lizard")
Group: ornithischians
Period: Early Cretaceous
Size and weight: 80cm (32in) long, 3kg (6.6lb)
Location: China
Description: Herbivore with a beak, and leaf-shaped teeth. It walked on two legs.

JIANGSHANOSAURUS ("Jiangshan lizard")
Group: saurischians, sauropodomorphs, sauropods
Period: Early Cretaceous
Size and weight: 20m (66ft) long, 12 tonnes (13 tons)
Location: China
Description: Long-necked herbivore with slim legs. It walked on four legs and might have been similar to Alamosaurus.

JINGSHANOSAURUS ("Jingshan lizard")
Group: saurischians, sauropodomorphs, prosauropods
Period: Early Jurassic
Size and weight: 10m (33ft) long, 3 tonnes (3.3 tons)
Location: China
Description: Long-necked herbivore with a sturdy body and a sloping snout. It walked on four legs.

JINZHOUSAURUS ("Jinzhou lizard")
Group: ornithischians, ornithopods, iguanodonts
Period: Early Cretaceous
Size and weight: 7m (23ft) long, 1.5 tonnes (1.7 tons)
Location: China
Description: Herbivore with grinding teeth. It could walk on two or four legs.

JOBARIA ("for Jobar")
Group: saurischians, sauropodomorphs, sauropods
Period: Early Cretaceous
Size and weight: 18m (59ft) long, 20 tonnes (22 tons)
Location: western Africa
Description: Long-necked herbivore with huge nostrils. It walked on four legs.

KAIJIANGOSAURUS ("Kai River lizard")
Group: saurischians, theropods and possibly coelurosaurs
Period: Middle Jurassic
Size and weight: 7m (23ft) long, 1 tonne (1.1 tons)
Location: China
Description: Large predator that walked on two legs. It might have been similar to Gasosaurus.

KAKURU ("ancestral servant")
Group: saurischians, theropods, coelurosaurs
Period: Late Cretaceous
Size and weight: 2.5m (8ft) long, 23kg (50lb)
Location: Australia
Description: Predator that walked on two legs. It's known only from its slim back leg bones.

KELMAYISAURUS ("Karamay lizard")
Group: saurischians, theropods and possibly allosaurs
Period: Early Cretaceous
Size and weight: 7m (23ft) long, 1 tonne (1.1 tons)
Location: China
Description: Large predator that walked on two legs. It might have been similar to Allosaurus.

KENTROSAURUS ("sharp-point lizard")
Group: ornithischians, thyreophorans, stegosaurs
Period: Late Jurassic
Size and weight: 4m (13ft) long, 320kg (705lb)
Location: eastern Africa
Description: Herbivore with plates sticking up from its neck, back and tail. It walked on four legs.

KHAAN ("ruler")
Group: saurischians, theropods, coelurosaurs
Period: Late Cretaceous
Size and weight: 1m (3ft) long, 4kg (8.8lb)
Location: Mongolia
Description: Toothless omnivore with a short skull shaped like a parrot's skull. It had long arms and a short tail, and it walked on two legs.

KLAMELISAURUS ("Klameli lizard")
Group: saurischians, sauropodomorphs, sauropods
Period: Middle Jurassic
Size and weight: 17m (56ft) long, 15 tonnes (17 tons)
Location: China
Description: Long-necked herbivore that walked on four legs. It had spoon-shaped teeth and might have had a ridge along its back.

KOPARION ("scalpel")
Group: saurischians, theropods, coelurosaurs
Period: Late Jurassic
Size and weight: 1m (3ft) long, 6kg (13lb)
Location: USA
Description: Small predator known only from fossilized teeth. It walked on two legs and might have been similar to Troodon.

KOTASAURUS ("Kota lizard")
Group: saurischians, sauropodomorphs, sauropods
Period: Early Jurassic
Size and weight: 18m (59ft) long, 8.5 tonnes (9.4 tons)
Location: India
Description: Primitive herbivore that walked on four legs. It had a long neck and spoon-shaped teeth.

KRITOSAURUS ("separated lizard")
Group: ornithischians, ornithopods, iguanodonts
Period: Late Cretaceous
Size and weight: 6.5m (21ft) long, 1.9 tonnes (2.1 tons)
Location: USA
Description: Herbivore with a bump on its nose, and a beak shaped like a duck's beak. It could walk on two or four legs.

KULCERATOPS ("lake horned face")
Group: ornithischians, marginocephalians, ceratopsians
Period: Early Cretaceous
Size and weight: 2m (7ft) long, 50kg (110lb)

Location: Uzbekistan
Description: Herbivore with horns on its face, a neck frill and teeth well-suited to shearing through vegetation. It walked on four legs.

LABOCANIA ("for La Bocana")
Group: saurischians, theropods and possibly coelurosaurs
Period: Late Cretaceous
Size and weight: 8m (26ft) long, 1.5 tonnes (1.7 tons)
Location: Mexico
Description: Predator with a large, heavy skull. It walked on two legs. Not much is known about it.

LAEVISUCHUS ("light crocodile")
Group: saurischians, theropods, neoceratosaurs
Period: Late Cretaceous
Size and weight: 1m (3ft) long, 4kg (8.8lb)
Location: India
Description: Small predator that walked on two legs. It might have been similar to Noasaurus and probably had slim limbs.

LAMBEOSAURUS ("Lambe's lizard")
Group: ornithischians, ornithopods, iguanodonts
Period: Late Cretaceous
Size and weight: 9m (30ft) long, 4.5 tonnes (5 tons)
Location: Canada and Mexico
Description: Large herbivore with a beak and a head crest. It could walk on two or four legs.

LAMETASAURUS ("Lameta lizard")
Group: saurischians, theropods, neoceratosaurs
Period: Late Cretaceous
Size and weight: 7.5m (25ft) long, 1 tonne (1.1 tons)
Location: India
Description: Predator that walked on two legs. It might have had bony ridges above its eyes.

LANASAURUS ("woolly lizard")
Group: ornithischians, heterodontosaurids
Period: Early Jurassic
Size and weight: 1m (3ft) long, 5kg (11lb)
Location: South Africa
Description: Small omnivore with fang-like front teeth. It could walk on two or four legs.

LAOSAURUS ("fossil lizard")
Group: ornithischians, ornithopods, hypsilophodontids
Period: Late Jurassic
Size and weight: 1.5m (5ft) long, 9kg (20lb)
Location: USA and Canada
Description: Small herbivore with a beak, short hands and long legs. It walked on two legs and was similar to Hypsilophodon.

LAPLATASAURUS ("La Plata lizard")
Group: saurischians, sauropodomorphs, sauropods
Period: Late Cretaceous
Size and weight: 18m (59ft) long, 11 tonnes (12 tons)
Location: Argentina and Uruguay
Description: Long-necked herbivore with column-like legs and plates on its back. It walked on four legs.

LAPPARENTOSAURUS ("Lapparent's lizard")
Group: saurischians, sauropodomorphs, sauropods
Period: Middle Jurassic
Size and weight: 16m (53ft) long, 20 tonnes (22 tons)
Location: Madagascar
Description: Large herbivore with column-like legs and a long neck. It walked on four legs.

LEAELLYNASAURA ("Leaellyn's lizard")
Group: ornithischians, ornithopods, hypsilophodontids
Period: Early Cretaceous
Size and weight: 1.5m (5ft) long, 9kg (20lb)
Location: Australia
Description: Small herbivore with long limbs and a beak. It had large eyes and walked on two legs.

LEPTOCERATOPS ("small horned face")
Group: ornithischians, marginocephalians, ceratopsians
Period: Late Cretaceous
Size and weight: 2.5m (8ft) long, 120kg (265lb)
Location: USA and Canada
Description: Herbivore with a short tail, a beak and a huge head. It walked on four legs.

LESOTHOSAURUS ("Lesotho lizard")
Group: ornithischians
Period: Early Jurassic
Size and weight: 1m (3ft) long, 4kg (8.8lb)
Location: southern Africa
Description: Dinosaur with a beak and a long snout. It was either a herbivore or an omnivore, and had slim hind legs. It walked on two legs.

LESSEMSAURUS ("Lessem's lizard")
Group: saurischians, sauropodomorphs, prosauropods
Period: Late Triassic
Size and weight: 10m (33ft) long, 3 tonnes (3.3 tons)
Location: Argentina
Description: Large herbivore with column-like hind legs, a long neck and a ridge along its back. It walked on four legs.

LEXOVISAURUS ("Lexovian lizard")
Group: ornithischians, thyreophorans, stegosaurs
Period: Middle and Late Jurassic
Size and weight: 5m (16ft) long, 1.1 tonnes (1.2 tons)
Location: England and France
Description: Herbivore with tough plates sticking up from its neck, back and tail. It had spikes along its tail and on its shoulders, and it walked on four legs.

LIAOCERATOPS ("Liaoning horned face")
Group: ornithischians, marginocephalians, ceratopsians
Period: Early Cretaceous
Size and weight: 90cm (35in) long, 5kg (11lb)
Location: China
Description: Small herbivore with a short neck frill and narrow beak. It probably walked on two legs.

LIAONINGOSAURUS ("Liaoning lizard")
Group: ornithischians, thyreophorans, ankylosaurs
Period: Early Cretaceous
Size and weight: 34cm (13in) long, 1kg (2lb)
Location: China
Description: Small, plated herbivore known only from one skeleton that belonged to a young animal. It walked on four legs.

LIGABUEINO ("Ligabue's little one")
Group: saurischians, theropods, neoceratosaurs
Period: Early Cretaceous
Size and weight: 1m (3ft) long, 4kg (8.8lb)
Location: Argentina
Description: Small predator that probably had slim limbs and a straight neck. It walked on two legs and might have been similar to Noasaurus.

LILIENSTERNUS ("for Lilienstern")
Group: saurischians, theropods, coelophysoids
Period: Late Triassic
Size and weight: 5m (16ft) long, 130kg (290lb)
Location: Germany
Description: Predator with a slim body and a skull similar to Coelophysis' skull. It walked on two legs.

LIRAINOSAURUS ("slender lizard")
Group: saurischians, sauropodomorphs, sauropods
Period: Late Cretaceous
Size and weight: 12m (39ft) long, 6 tonnes (6.6 tons)
Location: Spain
Description: Large herbivore with a long neck and plates on its back. It walked on four legs.

LOPHORHOTHON ("crested nose")
Group: ornithischians, ornithopods, iguanodonts
Period: Late Cretaceous
Size and weight: 8m (26ft) long, 3.2 tonnes (3.5 tons)
Location: USA
Description: Herbivore with a beak and a bump on its snout. It walked on two or four legs.

LOSILLASAURUS ("Losilla lizard")
Group: saurischians, sauropodomorphs, sauropods
Period: Early Cretaceous
Size and weight: 23m (75ft) long, 16 tonnes (18 tons)
Location: Spain
Description: Herbivore with a long neck and tail. It walked on four legs and was similar to Diplodocus.

LOURINHANOSAURUS ("Lourinhã lizard")
Group: saurischians, theropods, allosaurs
Period: Late Jurassic

Size and weight: 4m (13ft) long, 180kg (395lb)
Location: Portugal
Description: Predator that walked on two legs. It might have been similar to Sinraptor or Allosaurus.

LOURINHASAURUS ("Lourinhã lizard")
Group: saurischians, sauropodomorphs, sauropods
Period: Late Jurassic
Size and weight: 17m (56ft) long, 16 tonnes (18 tons)
Location: Portugal
Description: Long-necked herbivore that might have been similar to Camarasaurus. It walked on four legs.

LUCIANOSAURUS ("Lucian lizard")
Group: ornithischians
Period: Late Jurassic
Size and weight: 1m (3ft) long, 4kg (8.8lb)
Location: USA
Description: Dinosaur known only from its teeth. It was either a herbivore or an omnivore and might have been similar to Lesothosaurus. It walked on two legs.

LUFENGOSAURUS ("Lufeng lizard")
Group: saurischians, sauropodomorphs, prosauropods
Period: Late Triassic
Size and weight: 6m (20ft) long, 1 tonne (1.1 tons)
Location: China
Description: Long-necked herbivore with a long tail. It could walk on two or four legs.

LURDUSAURUS ("heavy lizard")
Group: ornithischians, ornithopods, iguanodonts
Period: Early Cretaceous
Size and weight: 9m (30ft) long, 5 tonnes (5.5 tons)
Location: western Africa
Description: Herbivore with a large body, stout limbs, a beak and spike-shaped thumbs. It could walk on two or four legs.

LYCORHINUS ("wolf snout")
Group: ornithischians, heterodontosaurids
Period: Early Jurassic
Size and weight: 1m (3ft) long, 5kg (11lb)
Location: South Africa
Description: Small omnivore with fang-like teeth at the front of its jaws. It could walk on two or four legs.

MACRUROSAURUS ("long-tailed lizard")
Group: saurischians, sauropodomorphs, sauropods
Period: Early Cretaceous
Size and weight: 18m (59ft) long, 11 tonnes (12 tons)
Location: England
Description: Long-necked herbivore with column-like legs. It walked on four legs.

MAGNOSAURUS ("large lizard")
Group: saurischians, theropods, and possibly spinosaurs
Period: Middle Jurassic
Size and weight: 5m (16ft) long, 220kg (485lb)
Location: England
Description: Predator that probably had short arms and a long skull. It walked on two legs.

MAGYAROSAURUS ("Magyar lizard")
Group: saurischians, sauropodomorphs, sauropods
Period: Late Cretaceous
Size and weight: 5m (16ft) long, 1 tonne (1.1 tons)
Location: eastern Europe
Description: Herbivore with a long neck and protective plates on its back. It walked on four legs.

MAIASAURA ("good mother lizard")
Group: ornithischians, ornithopods, iguanodonts
Period: Late Cretaceous
Size and weight: 9m (30ft) long, 4.5 tonnes (5 tons)
Location: USA
Description: Herbivore with a beak shaped like a duck's beak, and a crest above its eyes. It could walk on two or four legs.

MAJUNGATHOLUS ("Majunga dome")
Group: saurischians, theropods, neoceratosaurs
Period: Late Cretaceous
Size and weight: 8m (26ft) long, 1.1 tonnes (1.2 tons)
Location: Madagascar
Description: Long-limbed predator with a horn on its forehead. It walked on two legs.

MALAWISAURUS ("Malawi lizard")
Group: saurischians, sauropodomorphs, sauropods
Period: Early Cretaceous
Size and weight: 18m (59ft) long, 11 tonnes (12 tons)
Location: eastern Africa
Description: Large, long-necked herbivore with a small head and tough plates on its back. It walked on four legs.

MALEEVUS ("for Maleev")
Group: ornithischians, thyreophorans, ankylosaurs
Period: Late Cretaceous
Size and weight: 5m (16ft) long, 700kg (1,540lb)
Location: Mongolia
Description: Plated herbivore that walked on four legs. It had a box-shaped skull and a club at the end of its tail.

MAMENCHISAURUS ("Mamenchi lizard")
Group: saurischians, sauropodomorphs, sauropods
Period: Late Jurassic
Size and weight: 20m (66ft) long, 14 tonnes (15 tons)
Location: China
Description: Herbivore with an unusually long neck. It had long legs, a small, box-shaped head and it walked on four legs.

MARSHOSAURUS ("Marsh's lizard")
Group: saurischians, theropods, and possibly allosaurs
Period: Late Jurassic
Size and weight: 5m (16ft) long, 280kg (620lb)
Location: USA
Description: Predator with short, powerful arms. It walked on two legs and might have been similar to Allosaurus.

MASIAKASAURUS ("Masiaka lizard")
Group: saurischians, theropods, neoceratosaurs
Period: Late Cretaceous
Size and weight: 2m (7ft) long, 12kg (26lb)
Location: Madagascar
Description: Small predator with long front teeth that stuck out horizontally. It walked on two legs.

MASSOSPONDYLUS ("elongated vertebra")
Group: saurischians, sauropodomorphs, prosauropods
Period: Late Triassic
Size and weight: 4m (13ft) long, 130kg (290lb)
Location: southern Africa, Argentina and the USA
Description: Long-necked omnivore with large, curved thumb claws and a small head. It could walk on two or four legs.

MEGALOSAURUS ("great lizard")
Group: saurischians, theropods, spinosaurs
Period: Middle Jurassic
Size and weight: 7m (23ft) long, 1 tonne (1.1 tons)
Location: England
Description: Predator with short arms and backward-curving teeth. It walked on two legs.

MEGARAPTOR ("large thief")
Group: saurischians, theropods, coelurosaurs
Period: Late Cretaceous
Size and weight: 8m (26ft) long, 600kg (1,320lb)
Location: Argentina
Description: Predator with a large curved claw on each second toe. It walked on two legs.

MELANOROSAURUS ("Black Mountain lizard")
Group: saurischians, sauropodomorphs, prosauropods
Period: Late Triassic
Size and weight: 12m (39ft) long, 6 tonnes (6.6 tons)
Location: South Africa
Description: Large herbivore with a long neck and column-like hind legs. It walked on four legs.

METRIACANTHOSAURUS ("moderately spined lizard")
Group: saurischians, theropods, spinosaurs
Period: Late Jurassic
Size and weight: 7m (23ft) long, 1 tonne (1.1 tons)
Location: England
Description: Predator with short arms and a tall ridge along its back. It walked on two legs.

MICROCERATOPS ("small horned face")
Group: ornithischians, marginocephalians, ceratopsians

Period: Late Cretaceous
Size and weight: 75cm (30in) long, 2kg (4.4lb)
Location: China
Description: Herbivore with a beak, a short neck frill and wide cheeks. It was small and slim and could walk on two or four legs.

MICROPACHYCEPHALOSAURUS ("small thick-headed lizard")
Group: ornithischians, marginocephalians, pachycephalosaurs
Period: Late Cretaceous
Size and weight: 60cm (24in) long, 2kg (4.4lb)
Location: China
Description: Tiny herbivore with a broad body and a skull with a thick, flat top. It walked on two legs.

MICRORAPTOR ("small thief")
Group: saurischians, theropods, coelurosaurs
Period: Early Cretaceous
Size and weight: 30cm (12in) long, 350g (0.8lb)
Location: China
Description: Tiny bird-like predator with long arms, a stiff tail and curved foot claws. It walked on two legs.

MICROVENATOR ("small thief")
Group: saurischians, theropods, coelurosaurs
Period: Early Cretaceous
Size and weight: 1.5m (5ft) long, 11kg (24lb)
Location: USA
Description: Short-tailed dinosaur that was either a herbivore or an omnivore. It walked on two legs.

MINMI ("Minmi")
Group: ornithischians, thyreophorans, ankylosaurs
Period: Early Cretaceous
Size and weight: 3m (10ft) long, 60kg (130lb)
Location: Australia
Description: Herbivore with a beak, and plates on its belly, back and tail. It walked on four legs.

MONKONOSAURUS ("Monko lizard")
Group: ornithischians, thyreophorans, stegosaurs
Period: Late Jurassic and Early Cretaceous
Size and weight: 4.5m (15ft) long, 650kg (1,430lb)
Location: Tibet
Description: Herbivore with plates and spikes along its neck, back and tail. It walked on four legs.

MONOCLONIUS ("single sprout")
Group: ornithischians, marginocephalians, ceratopsians
Period: Late Cretaceous
Size and weight: 5m (16ft) long, 1.1 tonnes (1.2 tons)
Location: USA and Canada
Description: Herbivore with a beak, a long nose horn and a short neck frill. It walked on four legs.

MONOLOPHOSAURUS ("single crested lizard")
Group: saurischians, theropods, allosaurs
Period: Middle Jurassic
Size and weight: 6m (20ft) long, 600kg (1,320lb)
Location: China
Description: Predator with a hollow head crest and sharp teeth. It walked on two legs.

MONONYKUS ("one claw")
Group: saurischians, theropods, coelurosaurs
Period: Late Cretaceous
Size and weight: 1m (3ft) long, 3kg (6.6lb)
Location: Mongolia
Description: Feathered predator with a head shaped like a bird's head and short arms. It was an omnivore and it walked on two legs.

MONTANOCERATOPS ("Montana horned face")
Group: ornithischians, marginocephalians, ceratopsians
Period: Late Cretaceous
Size and weight: 1.8m (6ft) long, 50kg (110lb)
Location: USA
Description: Herbivore with a beak, a short neck frill and a small nose horn. It walked on four legs.

MUSSAURUS ("mouse lizard")
Group: saurischians, sauropodomorphs, prosauropods
Period: Late Triassic
Size and weight: Possibly 3m (10ft) long, 85kg (190lb)
Location: Argentina
Description: Long-necked herbivore known only from its eggs and tiny babies. It could walk on two or four legs.

MUTTABURRASAURUS ("Muttaburra lizard")
Group: ornithischians, ornithopods, iguanodonts
Period: Late Cretaceous
Size and weight: 9m (30ft) long, 4.1 tonnes (4.5 tons)
Location: Australia
Description: Herbivore with a toothless beak and grinding teeth. It had a thick crest on its snout and it could walk on two or four legs.

MYMOORAPELTA ("Mygatt and Moore's shield")
Group: ornithischians, thyreophorans, ankylosaurs
Period: Late Jurassic
Size and weight: 3m (10ft) long, 430kg (960lb)
Location: USA
Description: Herbivore with spikes on its tail and plates on its back and sides. It walked on four legs.

NAASHOIBITOSAURUS ("Naashoibito lizard")
Group: ornithischians, ornithopods, iguanodonts
Period: Late Cretaceous
Size and weight: 6.5m (21ft) long, 1.9 tonnes (2.1 tons)
Location: USA
Description: Herbivore with a beak shaped like a duck's beak, and a bump on its nose. It could walk on two or four legs.

NANOSAURUS ("pygmy lizard")
Group: ornithischians, ornithopods, hypsilophodontids
Period: Late Jurassic
Size and weight: 90cm (35in) long, 4kg (8.8lb)
Location: USA
Description: Tiny herbivore with a beak, short hands and long legs. It was similar to Hypsilophodon and walked on two legs.

NANSHIUNGOSAURUS ("Nanxiong lizard")
Group: saurischians, theropods, coelurosaurs
Period: Late Cretaceous
Size and weight: 6m (20ft) long, 300kg (660lb)
Location: China
Description: Omnivore with long hand claws, a broad belly and a short tail. It was similar to Erlikosaurus and walked on two legs.

NANYANGOSAURUS ("Nanyang lizard")
Group: ornithischians, ornithopods, iguanodonts
Period: Early Cretaceous
Size and weight: 4.5m (15ft) long, 260kg (570lb)
Location: China
Description: Herbivore with grinding teeth and a toothless beak shaped like a duck's beak. It could walk on two or four legs.

NEDCOLBERTIA ("for Ned Colbert")
Group: saurischians, theropods, coelurosaurs
Period: Early Cretaceous
Size and weight: 3m (10ft) long, 40kg (88lb)
Location: USA
Description: Predator with long, slim hind legs and sharp claws on its hands. It walked on two legs.

NEIMONGOSAURUS ("Nei Mongol lizard")
Group: saurischians, theropods, coelurosaurs
Period: Late Cretaceous
Size and weight: 2.5m (8ft) long, 100kg (220lb)
Location: China
Description: Long-necked dinosaur with long arms and leaf-shaped teeth. It was either a herbivore or an omnivore and walked on two legs.

NEMEGTOSAURUS ("Nemegt lizard")
Group: saurischians, sauropodomorphs, sauropods
Period: Late Cretaceous
Size and weight: 12m (39ft) long, 10 tonnes (11 tons)
Location: Mongolia
Description: Large, long-necked herbivore with pencil-like teeth and a wide mouth. It walked on four legs.

NEOVENATOR ("new hunter")
Group: saurischians, theropods, allosaurs
Period: Early Cretaceous
Size and weight: 7.5m (25ft) long, 1 tonne (1.1 tons)
Location: England
Description: Predator with a ridged skull. It was similar to Allosaurus and walked on two legs.

NEUQUENSAURUS ("Neuquén lizard")
Group: saurischians, sauropodomorphs, sauropods
Period: Late Cretaceous
Size and weight: 12m (39ft) long, 6 tonnes (6.6 tons)
Location: Argentina
Description: Herbivore with column-like legs and a long neck. It walked on four legs and probably had protective plates on its body.

NIGERSAURUS ("Niger lizard")
Group: saurischians, sauropodomorphs, sauropods
Period: Early Cretaceous
Size and weight: 15m (49ft) long, 7 tonnes (7.7 tons)
Location: Niger
Description: Long-necked herbivore that walked on four legs. Its mouth was wider than the rest of its head and was filled with around 600 thin teeth.

NIOBRARASAURUS ("Niobrara lizard")
Group: ornithischians, thyreophorans, ankylosaurs
Period: Late Cretaceous
Size and weight: 6m (20ft) long, 1.2 tonnes (1.3 tons)
Location: USA
Description: Herbivore with protective plates, a long flexible tail, wide hips and short legs. It walked on four legs.

NIPPONOSAURUS ("Japanese lizard")
Group: ornithischians, ornithopods, iguanodonts
Period: Late Cretaceous
Size and weight: 5m (16ft) long, 1.1 tonnes (1.2 tons)
Location: Russia
Description: Herbivore with grinding teeth and a beak shaped like a duck's beak. It could walk on two or four legs.

NOASAURUS ("northwestern Argentina lizard")
Group: saurischians, theropods, neoceratosaurs
Period: Late Cretaceous
Size and weight: 2m (7ft) long, 15kg (33lb)
Location: Argentina
Description: Small predator with a raised claw on each foot and a rather straight neck. It walked on two legs.

NODOCEPHALOSAURUS ("knob-headed lizard")
Group: ornithischians, thyreophorans, ankylosaurs
Period: Late Cretaceous
Size and weight: 6m (20ft) long, 1.2 tonnes (1.3 tons)
Location: USA
Description: Herbivore known only from its broad, plate-covered skull. It had a beak, and walked on four legs.

NODOSAURUS ("knob lizard")
Group: ornithischians, thyreophorans, ankylosaurs
Period: Late Cretaceous
Size and weight: 6m (20ft) long, 1.2 tonnes (1.3 tons)
Location: USA
Description: Plated herbivore with a short neck and legs and a long, flexible tail. It had a narrow head with a pointed snout. It walked on four legs and had broad hips.

NOMINGIA ("for Nomingiin")
Group: saurischians, theropods, coelurosaurs
Period: Late Cretaceous
Size and weight: 2.5m (8ft) long, 30kg (66lb)
Location: Mongolia
Description: Dinosaur that was either a herbivore or an omnivore and walked on two legs. It was similar to Oviraptor, but it had tail bones that were fused together.

NOTHRONYCHUS ("slothful claw")
Group: saurischians, theropods, coelurosaurs
Period: Late Cretaceous
Size and weight: 5m (16ft) long, 180kg (400lb)
Location: USA
Description: Omnivore that was similar to Erlikosaurus. It had long claws on its hands, a broad belly and a short tail. It walked on two legs.

NOTOHYPSILOPHODON ("southern Hypsilophus tooth")
Group: ornithischians, ornithopods, hypsilophodontids
Period: Late Cretaceous
Size and weight: 1.5m (5ft) long, 9kg (20lb)
Location: Argentina
Description: Herbivore with a beak, slim hind legs and short arms. It walked on two legs.

NQWEBASAURUS ("Kirkwood lizard")
Group: saurischians, theropods, coelurosaurs
Period: Early Cretaceous
Size and weight: 1m (3ft) long, 4kg (8.8lb)
Location: South Africa
Description: Predator with three fingers on each hand and slim, curved claws. It walked on two legs.

NUTHETES ("monitor")
Group: saurischians, theropods, coelurosaurs
Period: Early Cretaceous
Size and weight: 1m (3ft) long, 3kg (6.6lb)
Location: England
Description: Small predator known only from its teeth. It walked on two legs and probably had long arms and a stiff tail.

OHMDENOSAURUS ("Ohmden lizard")
Group: saurischians, sauropodomorphs, sauropods
Period: Early Jurassic
Size and weight: 4m (13ft) long, 150kg (330lb)
Location: Germany
Description: Long-necked herbivore that might have been similar to Vulcanodon. It walked on four legs.

OMEISAURUS ("Emei lizard")
Group: saurischians, sauropodomorphs, sauropods
Period: Late Jurassic
Size and weight: 18m (59ft) long, 8.5 tonnes (9.4 tons)
Location: China
Description: Herbivore with a very long neck, a box-shaped skull and long legs. It walked on four legs.

OPISTHOCOELICAUDIA ("tail cupped behind")
Group: saurischians, sauropodomorphs, sauropods
Period: Late Cretaceous
Size and weight: 12m (39ft) long, 10 tonnes (11 tons)
Location: Mongolia
Description: Long-necked herbivore that walked on four legs. The shape of its tail bones suggests it could rear up on its hind legs, using its tail for support.

ORNATOTHOLUS ("decorated dome")
Group: ornithischians, marginocephalians, pachycephalosaurs
Period: Late Cretaceous
Size and weight: 2.5m (8ft) long, 60kg (130lb)
Location: Canada
Description: Herbivore with a beak, a wide body and short arms. It walked on two legs.

ORNITHODESMUS ("bird link")
Group: saurischians, theropods, coelurosaurs
Period: Early Cretaceous
Size and weight: 1.5m (5ft) long, 5kg (11lb)
Location: England
Description: Predator known only from its hipbones. It walked on two legs and might have been similar to Velociraptor.

ORNITHOLESTES ("bird thief")
Group: saurischians, theropods, coelurosaurs
Period: Late Jurassic
Size and weight: 2m (7ft) long, 13kg (29lb)
Location: USA
Description: Small predator with three long fingers on each hand, a small skull and a long tail. It walked on two legs.

ORNITHOMIMUS ("bird mimic")
Group: saurischians, theropods, coelurosaurs
Period: Late Cretaceous
Size and weight: 3m (10ft) long, 110kg (240lb)
Location: USA and Canada
Description: Fast-running omnivore with a toothless beak and long hands. It walked on two legs.

ORODROMEUS ("mountain runner")
Group: ornithischians, ornithopods, hypsilophodontids
Period: Late Cretaceous
Size and weight: 2m (7ft) long, 13kg (29lb)
Location: USA
Description: Herbivore with a beak, a stiff tail, short arms and five fingers on each hand. It walked on two legs.

OTHNIELIA ("for Othniel")
Group: ornithischians, ornithopods, hypsilophodontids
Period: Late Jurassic
Size and weight: 3m (10ft) long, 16kg (35lb)
Location: USA
Description: Dinosaur that was either a herbivore or an omnivore. It had a beak, and walked on two legs.

OURANOSAURUS ("fearless lizard")
Group: ornithischians, ornithopods, iguanodonts
Period: Early Cretaceous
Size and weight: 6m (20ft) long, 1.1 tonnes (1.2 tonnes)
Location: northern Africa
Description: Herbivore with a beak like a duck's and a sail on its back. It could walk on two or four legs.

OVIRAPTOR ("egg thief")
Group: saurischians, theropods, coelurosaurs
Period: Late Cretaceous
Size and weight: 2.5m (8ft) long, 35kg (77lb)
Location: Mongolia
Description: Toothless omnivore with long arms and a skull shaped like a parrot's skull. It had a short tail and walked on two legs.

OZRAPTOR ("Australian thief")
Group: saurischians, theropods
Period: Middle Jurassic
Size and weight: 2.5m (8ft) long, 20kg (44lb)
Location: Australia
Description: Predator known only from a partial leg bone. It walked on two legs.

PACHYCEPHALOSAURUS ("thick-headed lizard")
Group: ornithischians, marginocephalians, pachycephalosaurs
Period: Late Cretaceous
Size and weight: 5m (16ft) long, 300kg (660lb)
Location: USA
Description: Herbivore with a beak, and lumps and spikes on its thick skull. It walked on two legs.

PACHYRHINOSAURUS ("thick nose lizard")
Group: ornithischians, marginocephalians, ceratopsians
Period: Late Cretaceous
Size and weight: 6m (20ft) long, 1.5 tonnes (1.6 tons)
Location: Canada
Description: Herbivore with a beak, a neck frill and a thick, bony pad on its nose. It walked on four legs.

PANOPLOSAURUS ("completely shielded lizard")
Group: ornithischians, thyreophorans, ankylosaurs
Period: Late Cretaceous
Size and weight: 7m (23ft) long, 1.5 tonnes (1.6 tons)
Location: USA and Canada
Description: Plated herbivore with forward-pointing shoulder spikes. It walked on four legs.

PARALITITAN ("tidal giant")
Group: saurischians, sauropodomorphs, sauropods
Period: Late Cretaceous
Size and weight: 27m (89ft) long, 78 tonnes (86 tons)
Location: Egypt
Description: Giant, long-necked herbivore with long, column-like legs. It walked on four legs.

PARANTHODON ("near flower tooth")
Group: ornithischians, thyreophorans, stegosaurs
Period: Early Cretaceous
Size and weight: 4.5m (15ft) long, 650kg (1,430lb)
Location: southern Africa
Description: Herbivore with plates and spikes sticking up from its neck, back and tail. It walked on four legs.

PARARHABDODON ("near fluted tooth")
Group: ornithischians, ornithopods, iguanodonts
Period: Late Cretaceous
Size and weight: 5m (16ft) long, 1 tonne (1.1 tons)
Location: Spain
Description: Herbivore with a beak shaped like a duck's beak and grinding teeth. It could walk on two or four legs.

PARASAUROLOPHUS ("near crested lizard")
Group: ornithischians, ornithopods, iguanodonts
Period: Late Cretaceous
Size and weight: 9m (30ft) long, 5 tonnes (5.5 tons)
Location: USA and Canada
Description: Herbivore with a beak and a curved, tube-like head crest. It could walk on two or four legs.

PARIVCURSOR ("small runner")
Group: saurischians, theropods, coelurosaurs
Period: Late Cretaceous
Size and weight: 1m (3ft) long, 3kg (6.6lb)
Location: Mongolia

Description: Feathered omnivore with a head shaped like a bird's head. It walked on two legs.

PARKSOSAURUS ("Parks' lizard")
Group: ornithischians, ornithopods, hypsilophodontids
Period: Late Cretaceous
Size and weight: 2.5m (8ft) long, 60kg (132lb)
Location: Canada
Description: Herbivore with a beak, slim hind legs, short arms and leaf-shaped teeth. It walked on two legs.

PATAGONYKUS ("Patagonian claw")
Group: saurischians, theropods, coelurosaurs
Period: Late Cretaceous
Size and weight: 2m (7ft) long, 6kg (13lb)
Location: Argentina
Description: Feathered omnivore with a head shaped like a bird's head and short arms. It was an omnivore and walked on two legs.

PATAGOSAURUS ("Patagonian lizard")
Group: saurischians, sauropodomorphs, sauropods
Period: Middle Jurassic
Size and weight: 15m (49ft) long, 9 tonnes (10 tons)
Location: Argentina
Description: Long-necked herbivore with spoon-shaped teeth. It was similar to Cetiosaurus and walked on four legs.

PAWPAWSAURUS ("Paw Paw lizard")
Group: ornithischians, thyreophorans, ankylosaurs
Period: Early Cretaceous
Size and weight: 5m (16ft) long, 700kg (1,545lb)
Location: USA
Description: Herbivore with blunt horns and a plated skull. It walked on four legs.

PEKINOSAURUS ("Pekin lizard")
Group: ornithischians
Period: Late Jurassic
Size and weight: 1m (3ft) long, 4kg (8.8lb)
Location: USA
Description: Dinosaur known only from its distinctive teeth. It was either a herbivore or an omnivore and it was probably similar to Lesothosaurus. It walked on two legs.

PELECANIMIMUS ("pelican mimic")
Group: saurischians, theropods, coelurosaurs
Period: Early Cretaceous
Size and weight: 2.5m (8ft) long, 25kg (55lb)
Location: Spain
Description: Omnivore with a long skull and around 200 small teeth. It had long arms and it walked on two legs.

PELLEGRINISAURUS ("Pellegrini lizard")
Group: saurischians, sauropodomorphs, sauropods
Period: Late Cretaceous
Size and weight: 25m (82ft) long, 20 tonnes (22 tons)
Location: Argentina
Description: Huge, long-necked herbivore with a long, flexible tail and a broad body. It walked on four legs.

PELOROSAURUS ("colossal lizard")
Group: saurischians, sauropodomorphs, sauropods
Period: Early Cretaceous
Size and weight: 16m (53ft) long, 20 tonnes (22 tons)
Location: England, Portugal and France
Description: Long-necked herbivore with very long, slim front legs. It walked on four legs.

PENTACERATOPS ("five-horned face")
Group: ornithischians, marginocephalians, ceratopsians
Period: Late Cretaceous
Size and weight: 7.5m (25ft) long, 2.2 tonnes (2.4 tons)
Location: USA
Description: Large herbivore with a frill, three very long horns and a beak. It walked on four legs.

PHAEDROLOSAURUS ("nimble dragon")
Group: saurischians, theropods, coelurosaurs
Period: Early Cretaceous
Size and weight: 2m (7ft) long, 15kg (33lb)
Location: China
Description: Bird-like predator with long arms and large claws on its feet. It walked on two legs.

PHUWIANGOSAURUS ("Phu Wiang lizard")
Group: saurischians, sauropodomorphs, sauropods
Period: Early Cretaceous
Size and weight: 15m (49ft) long, 14 tonnes (15 tons)
Location: Thailand
Description: Large herbivore with a long, broad neck and wide body. It walked on four legs.

PHYLLODON ("leaf tooth")
Group: ornithischians, ornithopods, hypsilophodontids
Period: Late Jurassic
Size and weight: 90cm (35in) long, 4kg (8.8lb)
Location: Portugal
Description: Tiny herbivore known only from its leaf-shaped teeth. It walked on two legs and was probably similar to Hypsilophodon.

PIATNITZKYSAURUS ("Piatnitzky's lizard")
Group: saurischians, theropods, spinosaurs
Period: Middle Jurassic
Size and weight: 5m (16ft) long, 280kg (620lb)
Location: Argentina
Description: Predator with three fingers on each hand and horns above its eyes. It walked on two legs.

PINACOSAURUS ("plank lizard")
Group: ornithischians, thyreophorans, ankylosaurs
Period: Late Cretaceous
Size and weight: 5m (16ft) long, 700kg (1,545lb)
Location: China and Mongolia
Description: Plated herbivore with a box-shaped skull and a clubbed tail. It walked on four legs.

PISANOSAURUS ("Pisano's lizard")
Group: ornithischians
Period: Late Triassic
Size and weight: 1m (3ft) long, 7kg (15lb)
Location: Argentina
Description: Primitive herbivore with a beak and short arms. It walked on two legs.

PIVETEAUSAURUS ("Piveteau's lizard")
Group: saurischians, theropods, and possibly spinosaurs
Period: Middle Jurassic
Size and weight: 10m (33ft) long, 2 tonnes (2.2 tons)
Location: France
Description: Large predator that might have been similar to Megalosaurus. It walked on two legs. Not much is known about it.

PLANICOXA ("flat hip")
Group: ornithischians, ornithopods, iguanodonts
Period: Early Cretaceous
Size and weight: 7m (23ft) long, 1.5 tonnes (1.7 tons)
Location: USA
Description: Herbivore that could walk on two or four legs.

PLATEOSAURUS ("broad lizard")
Group: saurischians, sauropodomorphs, prosauropods
Period: Late Triassic
Size and weight: 7m (23ft) long, 800kg (1,765lb)
Location: Germany, Switzerland and France
Description: Long-necked herbivore with large thumb claws and a long tail. It could walk on two or four legs.

PLEUROCOELUS ("hollow-sided")
Group: saurischians, sauropodomorphs, sauropods
Period: Early Cretaceous
Size and weight: 13m (43ft) long, 7 tonnes (7.7 tons)
Location: USA
Description: Long-necked herbivore that walked on four legs. It had long, slim front legs.

POEKILOPLEURON ("varied ribs")
Group: saurischians, theropods, spinosaurs
Period: Middle Jurassic
Size and weight: 9m (30ft) long, 1 tonne (1.1 tons)
Location: France
Description: Predator with short arms and backward-curving teeth. It walked on two legs.

POLACANTHUS ("many spines")
Group: ornithischians, thyreophorans, ankylosaurs
Period: Early Cretaceous
Size and weight: 5m (16ft) long, 800kg (1,765lb)

Location: England and Spain
Description: Herbivore with triangular spikes on its tail, and plates on its back and sides. It walked on four legs.

PRENOCEPHALE ("sloping head")
Group: ornithischians, marginocephalians, pachycephalosaurs
Period: Late Cretaceous
Size and weight: 2m (7ft) long, 35kg (77lb)
Location: Mongolia
Description: Dinosaur with a dome-shaped skull and short arms. It was either a herbivore or an omnivore and walked on two legs.

PROBACTROSAURUS ("before club lizard")
Group: ornithischians, ornithopods, iguanodonts
Period: Late Cretaceous
Size and weight: 3.5m (11ft) long, 180kg (400lb)
Location: Mongolia
Description: Herbivore with a toothless beak shaped like a duck's beak, and grinding teeth. It walked on two or four legs.

PROCERATOSAURUS ("before horned lizard")
Group: saurischians, theropods, coelurosaurs
Period: Middle Jurassic
Size and weight: 1.5m (5ft) long, 5kg (11lb)
Location: England
Description: Predator with a narrow skull, a nose horn and curved, serrated teeth. It walked on two legs. It is one of the oldest-known coelurosaurs.

PROCOMPSOGNATHUS ("before elegant jaw")
Group: saurischians, theropods, coelophysoids
Period: Late Triassic
Size and weight: 1.2m (4ft) long, 2kg (4.4lb)
Location: Germany
Description: Small, slim predator with a long skull, sharp teeth and short arms. It walked on two legs.

PROSAUROLOPHUS ("before crested lizard")
Group: ornithischians, ornithopods, iguanodonts
Period: Late Cretaceous
Size and weight: 8m (26ft) long, 3.2 tonnes (3.5 tons)
Location: Canada and USA
Description: Herbivore with a beak shaped like a duck's beak. It could walk on two or four legs.

PROTARCHAEOPTERYX ("before ancient wing")
Group: saurischians, theropods, coelurosaurs
Period: Early Cretaceous
Size and weight: 1m (3ft) long, 4kg (8.8lb)
Location: China
Description: Small, feathered dinosaur with a short, skull, a beak and a short tail. It was either a herbivore or an omnivore and it walked on four legs.

PROTOCERATOPS ("first horned face")
Group: ornithischians, marginocephalians, ceratopsians
Period: Late Cretaceous
Size and weight: 1.4m (4.6ft) long, 24kg (53lb)
Location: Mongolia
Description: Herbivore with a narrow beak and a large neck frill. It walked on four legs.

PROTOGNATHOSAURUS ("first jaw lizard")
Group: saurischians, sauropodomorphs, sauropods
Period: Early Jurassic
Size and weight: 15m (49ft) long, 12 tonnes (13 tons)
Location: China
Description: Long-necked herbivore that might have been similar to Cetiosaurus. It walked on four legs.

PROTOHADROS ("first hadrosaur")
Group: ornithischians, ornithopods, iguanodonts
Period: Late Cretaceous
Size and weight: 7m (23ft) long, 2.2 tonnes (2.4 tons)
Location: USA
Description: Herbivore with a beak shaped like a duck's beak, and grinding teeth. It could walk on two or four legs.

PSITTACOSAURUS ("parrot lizard")
Group: ornithischians, marginocephalians, ceratopsians
Period: Late Cretaceous
Size and weight: 1.5m (5ft) long, 12kg (26lb)
Location: Mongolia, China and Thailand
Description: Herbivore with a skull shaped like a parrot's skull, and pointed cheeks. It could walk on two or four legs.

PUKYONGOSAURUS ("Pukyong lizard")
Group: saurischians, sauropodomorphs, sauropods
Period: Early Cretaceous
Size and weight: 10m (33ft) long, 8.5 tonnes (9.4 tons)
Location: South Korea
Description: Long-necked herbivore that probably had a blunt snout and slender legs. It walked on four legs. Not much is known about it.

PYRORAPTOR ("fire thief")
Group: saurischians, theropods, coelurosaurs
Period: Late Cretaceous
Size and weight: 2m (7ft) long, 15kg (33lb)
Location: France
Description: Bird-like predator with long arms and a large claw on each foot. It walked on two legs.

QANTASSAURUS ("Qantas lizard")
Group: ornithischians, ornithopods, hypsilophodontids
Period: Early Cretaceous
Size and weight: 1.5m (5ft) long, 10kg (22lb)
Location: Australia
Description: Herbivore with a beak, short arms, long hind legs and a long tail. It walked on two legs and had a shorter skull than other hypsilophodontids.

QINLINGOSAURUS ("Qin Ling lizard")
Group: saurischians, sauropodomorphs, sauropods
Period: Late Cretaceous
Size and weight: 15m (49ft) long, 12 tonnes (13 tons)
Location: China
Description: Long-necked herbivore known only from hipbones. It walked on four legs.

QUAESITOSAURUS ("extraordinary lizard")
Group: saurischians, sauropodomorphs, sauropods
Period: Late Cretaceous
Size and weight: 12m (39ft) long, 10 tonnes (11 tons)
Location: Mongolia
Description: Large, long-necked herbivore known only from its skull. It had pencil-shaped teeth and it walked on four legs.

QUILMESAURUS ("Quilmes lizard")
Group: saurischians, theropods, and possibly neoceratosaurs
Period: Late Cretaceous
Size and weight: 7.5m (25ft) long, 1 tonne (1.1 tons)
Location: Argentina
Description: Predator known only from leg bones. It walked on two legs and might have been similar to Abelisaurus.

RAPATOR ("plunderer")
Group: saurischians, theropods, coelurosaurs
Period: Early Cretaceous
Size and weight: 4m (13ft) long, 140kg (310lb)
Location: Australia
Description: Predator known only from one hand bone. It walked on two legs and might have been a giant relative of Mononykus.

RAPETOSAURUS ("Rapeto lizard")
Group: saurischians, sauropodomorphs, sauropods
Period: Late Cretaceous
Size and weight: 10m (33ft) long, 8 tonnes (8.8 tons)
Location: Madagascar
Description: Long-necked herbivore with a wide body and pencil-shaped teeth. It walked on four legs.

RAYOSOSAURUS ("Rayoso lizard")
Group: saurischians, sauropodomorphs, sauropods
Period: Late Cretaceous
Size and weight: 20m (66ft) long, 14 tonnes (15 tons)
Location: Argentina
Description: Herbivore with pencil-shaped teeth, a long neck and slim legs. It walked on four legs.

REBBACHISAURUS ("Rebbach lizard")
Group: saurischians, sauropodomorphs, sauropods
Period: Early Cretaceous
Size and weight: 20m (66ft) long, 14 tonnes (15 tons)
Location: northern Africa
Description: Large, long-necked herbivore with a long tail and a tall sail on its back. It walked on four legs.

REGNOSAURUS ("Regni lizard")
Group: ornithischians, thyreophorans, stegosaurs
Period: Early Cretaceous
Size and weight: 4.5m (15ft) long, 650kg (1,430lb)
Location: England
Description: Herbivore with plates and spikes sticking up along its neck, back and tail. It walked on four legs. Not much is known about it.

REVUELTOSAURUS ("Revuelto lizard")
Group: ornithischians
Period: Late Jurassic
Size and weight: 2.5m (8ft) long, 25kg (55lb)
Location: USA
Description: Dinosaur known only from its small teeth. It was probably similar to Lesothosaurus and it was either a herbivore or an omnivore. It walked on two legs.

RHABDODON ("fluted tooth")
Group: ornithischians, ornithopods, iguanodonts
Period: Late Cretaceous
Size and weight: 7m (23ft) long, 1 tonne (1.1 tons)
Location: France, Spain and eastern Europe
Description: Herbivore that walked on two legs. It had a beak, and might have been similar to Tenontosaurus.

RHOETOSAURUS ("Rhoetos lizard")
Group: saurischians, sauropodomorphs, sauropods
Period: Early Jurassic
Size and weight: 12m (39ft) long, 9 tonnes (10 tons)
Location: Australia
Description: Long-necked herbivore with long, sturdy legs and spoon-shaped teeth. It walked on four legs.

RICARDOESTESIA ("for Richard Estes")
Group: saurischians, theropods, coelurosaurs
Period: Late Cretaceous
Size and weight: 1.5m (5ft) long, 6kg (13lb)
Location: USA and Canada
Description: Bird-like predator with narrow jaws and pointed teeth. It walked on two legs.

RIOJASAURUS ("Rioja lizard")
Group: saurischians, sauropodomorphs, prosauropods
Period: Late Triassic
Size and weight: 10m (33ft) long, 3 tonnes (3.3 tons)
Location: Argentina
Description: Large, long-necked herbivore with column-like hind legs. It walked on four legs.

ROCASAURUS ("Roca lizard")
Group: saurischians, sauropodomorphs, sauropods
Period: Late Cretaceous
Size and weight: 9m (30ft) long, 4 tonnes (4.4 tons)
Location: Argentina
Description: Herbivore with a long neck and column-like legs. It walked on four legs.

RUEHLEIA ("for Rühle")
Group: saurischians, sauropodomorphs, prosauropods
Period: Late Triassic
Size and weight: 7m (23ft) long, 800kg (1,765lb)
Location: Germany
Description: Herbivore with a long neck and tail and large thumb claws. It could walk on two or four legs.

SAICHANIA ("beautiful one")
Group: ornithischians, thyreophorans, ankylosaurs
Period: Late Cretaceous
Size and weight: 7m (23ft) long, 1.4 tonnes (1.5 tons)
Location: Mongolia
Description: Herbivore with a tail club, and plates on its belly as well as its back. It had a box-shaped skull and it walked on four legs.

SALTASAURUS ("Salta lizard")
Group: saurischians, sauropodomorphs, sauropods
Period: Late Cretaceous
Size and weight: 12m (39ft) long, 6 tonnes (6.6 tons)
Location: Argentina
Description: Long-necked herbivore with broad hips, and plates covering its back. It walked on four legs.

SANTANARAPTOR ("Santana thief")
Group: saurischians, theropods, coelurosaurs
Period: Early Cretaceous

Size and weight: 2m (7ft) long, 13kg (29lb)
Location: Brazil
Description: Predator that had three fingers on each hand and walked on two legs. Not much is known about it.

SARCOLESTES ("flesh stealer")
Group: ornithischians, thyreophorans, ankylosaurs
Period: Middle Jurassic
Size and weight: 3m (10ft) long, 500kg (1,100lb)
Location: England
Description: Plated herbivore known only from one jaw. It had leaf-shaped teeth and walked on four legs.

SARCOSAURUS ("flesh lizard")
Group: saurischians, theropods, neoceratosaurs
Period: Early Jurassic
Size and weight: 3.5m (11ft) long, 100kg (220lb)
Location: England
Description: Predator that might have been similar to Ceratosaurus, but smaller. It walked on two legs.

SATURNALIA ("carnival")
Group: saurischians, sauropodomorphs
Period: Late Triassic
Size and weight: 1.5m (5ft) long, 9kg (20lb)
Location: Brazil
Description: Primitive sauropodomorph with a long neck and a small, pointed skull. It was an omnivore and could walk on two or four legs.

SAUROLOPHUS ("crested lizard")
Group: ornithischians, ornithopods, iguanodonts
Period: Late Cretaceous
Size and weight: 13m (43ft) long, 7 tonnes (7.7 tons)
Location: Canada and Mongolia
Description: Herbivore with a spike-shaped head crest. It had a toothless beak shaped like a duck's beak, and grinding teeth. It was one of the biggest hadrosaurs and could walk on two or four legs.

SAUROPELTA ("shield lizard")
Group: ornithischians, thyreophorans, ankylosaurs
Period: Early Cretaceous
Size and weight: 5m (16ft) long, 900kg (1,985lb)
Location: USA
Description: Plated herbivore with triangular spikes on its neck and shoulders. It walked on four legs.

SAUROPHAGANAX ("king of reptile eaters")
Group: saurischians, theropods, allosaurs
Period: Late Jurassic
Size and weight: 8m (26ft) long, 3 tonnes (3.3 tons)
Location: USA
Description: Predator that was similar to Allosaurus. It had three fingers on each hand and walked on two legs.

SAUROPOSEIDON ("Poseidon lizard")
Group: saurischians, sauropodomorphs, sauropods
Period: Early Cretaceous
Size and weight: 30m (98ft) long, 55 tonnes (61 tons)
Location: USA
Description: Huge, long-necked herbivore that was similar to Brachiosaurus. It walked on four legs.

SAURORNITHOIDES ("bird-like lizard")
Group: saurischians, theropods, coelurosaurs
Period: Late Cretaceous
Size and weight: 2m (7ft) long, 15kg (33lb)
Location: Mongolia
Description: Long-legged predator that was either a carnivore or an omnivore. It walked on two legs.

SAURORNITHOLESTES ("bird-like lizard stealer")
Group: saurischians, theropods, coelurosaurs
Period: Late Cretaceous
Size and weight: 1.5m (5ft) long, 5kg (11lb)
Location: Canada
Description: Predator with a stiffened tail. It walked on two legs and was similar to Velociraptor.

SCANSORIOPTERYX ("climbing wing")
Group: saurischians, theropods, coelurosaurs
Period: Early Cretaceous
Size and weight: 20cm (8in) long, 70g (0.2lb)
Location: China
Description: Tiny predator with long arms and a very long third finger on each hand. It walked on two legs.

SCELIDOSAURUS ("hind leg lizard")
Group: ornithischians, thyreophorans, ankylosaurs
Period: Early Jurassic
Size and weight: 3m (10ft) long, 64kg (140lb)
Location: England
Description: Herbivore that had a beak, and plates along its back and sides. It walked on four legs.

SCIPIONYX ("Scipio's claw")
Group: saurischians, theropods, coelurosaurs
Period: Early Cretaceous
Size and weight: 30cm (12in) long, 450g (1lb)
Location: Italy
Description: Very small predator with a large skull, sharp teeth and three fingers on each hand. It walked on two legs.

SCUTELLOSAURUS ("small shield lizard")
Group: ornithischians, thyreophorans
Period: Early Jurassic
Size and weight: 1.2m (4ft) long, 17kg (37lb)
Location: USA
Description: Herbivore with a long tail and rows of protective plates on its back and sides. It could walk on two or four legs.

SECERNOSAURUS ("separated lizard")
Group: ornithischians, ornithopods, iguanodonts
Period: Late Cretaceous
Size and weight: 3m (10ft) long, 450kg (990lb)
Location: Argentina
Description: Herbivore with a beak shaped like a duck's beak, and grinding teeth. It could walk on two or four legs.

SEGISAURUS ("Segi lizard")
Group: saurischians, theropods, coelophysoids
Period: Early Jurassic
Size and weight: 1.5m (5ft) long, 7kg (15lb)
Location: USA
Description: Predator with a slim body and long legs. It walked on two legs.

SEGNOSAURUS ("slow lizard")
Group: saurischians, theropods, coelurosaurs
Period: Late Cretaceous
Size and weight: 6.5m (21ft) long, 400kg (880lb)
Location: Mongolia
Description: Long-necked omnivore with long claws on its hands, a broad belly and a short tail. It walked on two legs.

SEISMOSAURUS ("earth shaker lizard")
Group: saurischians, sauropodomorphs, sauropods
Period: Late Jurassic
Size and weight: 34m (110ft) long, 30 tonnes (33 tons)
Location: USA
Description: Giant herbivore with a long neck and tail, and pencil-shaped teeth. It walked on four legs.

SELLOSAURUS ("saddle lizard")
Group: saurischians, sauropodomorphs
Period: Late Triassic
Size and weight: 3m (10ft) long, 85kg (185lb)
Location: Germany
Description: Herbivore with a long neck. It had large thumb claws and could walk on two or four legs.

SHAMOSAURUS ("desert lizard")
Group: ornithischians, thyreophorans, ankylosaurs
Period: Late Cretaceous
Size and weight: 6m (20ft) long, 1.3 tonnes (1.4 tons)
Location: Mongolia
Description: Plated herbivore with a narrow beak and small teeth. It walked on four legs.

SHANTUNGOSAURUS ("Shangdong lizard")
Group: ornithischians, ornithopods, iguanodonts
Period: Late Cretaceous
Size and weight: 17m (56ft) long, 15 tonnes (17 tons)
Location: China
Description: Large herbivore with a beak shaped like a duck's beak, and an especially large lower jaw. It could walk on two or four legs.

SHANXIA ("for Shanxi")
Group: ornithischians, thyreophorans, ankylosaurs
Period: Late Cretaceous
Size and weight: 5m (16ft) long, 700kg (1,545lb)
Location: China
Description: Plated herbivore with horns and a wide, flat skull. It walked on four legs.

SHANYANGOSAURUS ("Shangyang lizard")
Group: saurischians, theropods, coelurosaurs
Period: Late Cretaceous
Size and weight: 1.5m (5ft) long, 11kg (24lb)
Location: China
Description: Bird-like predator that might have been similar to Oviraptor. It walked on two legs.

SHUNOSAURUS ("Sichuan lizard")
Group: saurischians, sauropodomorphs, sauropods
Period: Middle Jurassic
Size and weight: 9m (30ft) long, 3 tonnes (3.3 tons)
Location: China
Description: Herbivore with a small head and a long tail with a spiked club. It walked on four legs.

SHUVOSAURUS ("Shuvo's lizard")
Group: saurischians, theropods, coelophysoids
Period: Late Triassic
Size and weight: 3m (10ft) long, 20kg (44lb)
Location: USA
Description: Toothless dinosaur that might have been similar to Coelophysis. It was either a herbivore or an omnivore and it walked on two legs.

SHUVUUIA ("bird")
Group: saurischians, theropods, coelurosaurs
Period: Late Cretaceous
Size and weight: 1m (3ft) long, 3kg (6.6lb)
Location: Mongolia
Description: Feathered omnivore with a head like a bird's. It had huge thumb claws and short arms, and it walked on two legs.

SIAMOSAURUS ("Siamese lizard")
Group: saurischians, theropods, spinosaurs
Period: Early Cretaceous
Size and weight: 8m (26ft) long, 1 tonne (1.1 tons)
Location: Thailand
Description: Predator known only from its teeth, which were similar to Spinosaurus'. It walked on two legs.

SIAMOTYRANNUS ("Siamese tyrant")
Group: saurischians, theropods, coelurosaurs
Period: Early Cretaceous
Size and weight: 6m (20ft) long, 700kg (1,545lb)
Location: Thailand
Description: Predator known only from its hipbones and tail. It might have been an early tyrannosaur. It walked on two legs.

SIGILMASSASAURUS ("Sijilmassa lizard")
Group: saurischians, theropods, and possibly allosaurs
Period: Early Cretaceous
Size and weight: 8m (26ft) long, 3 tonnes (3.3 tons)
Location: northern Africa
Description: Large predator that might have had thin arms and a slim neck. It walked on two legs.

SILVISAURUS ("forest lizard")
Group: ornithischians, thyreophorans, ankylosaurs
Period: Early Cretaceous
Size and weight: 4m (13ft) long, 400kg (880lb)
Location: USA
Description: Plated herbivore with a beak, and spines on its sides. It walked on four legs.

SINORNITHOIDES ("Chinese bird-like")
Group: saurischians, theropods, coelurosaurs
Period: Early Cretaceous
Size and weight: 1m (3ft) long, 5kg (11lb)
Location: China
Description: Long-legged predator with a slim skull and raised second toes. It walked on two legs and was either a carnivore or an omnivore.

SINORNITHOSAURUS ("Chinese bird-like lizard")
Group: saurischians, theropods, coelurosaurs
Period: Early Cretaceous
Size and weight: 1m (3ft) long, 4kg (8.8lb)
Location: China
Description: Feathered, bird-like predator with long arms, three fingers on each hand and a stiff tail. It walked on two legs.

SINOSAUROPTERYX ("Chinese lizard wing")
Group: saurischians, theropods, coelurosaurs
Period: Early Cretaceous
Size and weight: 1m (3ft) long, 3kg (6.6lb)
Location: China
Description: Small predator with short arms and large thumb claws. It walked on two legs.

SINOVENATOR ("Chinese hunter")
Group: saurischians, theropods, coelurosaurs
Period: Early Cretaceous
Size and weight: 1m (3ft) long, 6kg (13lb)
Location: China
Description: Small predator with long, slim hind legs and a stiff tail. It was similar to Troodon and it walked on two legs.

SINRAPTOR ("Chinese thief")
Group: saurischians, theropods, allosaurs
Period: Late Jurassic
Size and weight: 7m (23ft) long, 1 tonne (1.1 tons)
Location: China
Description: Predator with a large skull, a low ridge along its back and three fingers on each hand. It walked on two legs.

SONORASAURUS ("Sonora lizard")
Group: saurischians, sauropodomorphs, sauropods
Period: Early Cretaceous
Size and weight: 15m (49ft) long, 7 tonnes (7.7 tons)
Location: USA
Description: Long-necked herbivore with long, slim front legs. It walked on four legs.

SPHAEROTHOLUS ("Spherical dome")
Group: ornithischians, marginocephalians, pachycephalosaurs
Period: Late Cretaceous
Size and weight: 2m (7ft) long, 35kg (77lb)
Location: USA
Description: Dinosaur with a dome-shaped skull and short arms. It was either a herbivore or an omnivore and it walked on two legs.

SPINOSAURUS ("spine lizard")
Group: saurischians, theropods, spinosaurs
Period: Late Cretaceous
Size and weight: 15m (49ft) long, 4 tonnes (4.5 tons)
Location: northern Africa
Description: Giant predator with a skull that was shaped like a crocodile's skull. It had a tall sail on its back and it walked on two legs. It probably ate fish as well as other dinosaurs.

STAURIKOSAURUS ("Southern Cross lizard")
Group: saurischians, herrerasaurids
Period: Late Triassic
Size and weight: 2m (7ft) long, 14kg (31lb)
Location: Brazil
Description: Primitive predator with sharp claws and backward-curving teeth. It walked on two legs.

STEGOCERAS ("roofed horn")
Group: ornithischians, marginocephalians, pachycephalosaurs
Period: Late Cretaceous
Size and weight: 2m (7ft) long, 27kg (60lb)
Location: USA and Canada
Description: Herbivore with a beak, short arms and a thick, dome-shaped skull. It walked on two legs.

STEGOPELTA ("covered shield")
Group: ornithischians, thyreophorans, ankylosaurs
Period: Late Cretaceous
Size and weight: 6m (20ft) long, 1.2 tonnes (1.3 tons)
Location: USA
Description: Herbivore with a long, flexible tail, broad hips, protective plates and short legs. It walked on four legs.

STEGOSAURUS ("plated lizard")
Group: ornithischians, thyreophorans, stegosaurs
Period: Late Jurassic
Size and weight: 6.5m (21ft) long, 2.2 tonnes (2.4 tons)
Location: USA
Description: Herbivore with diamond-shaped plates sticking up from its neck, back and tail, and spikes at the end of its tail. It walked on four legs and its back legs were longer than its front legs.

STENOPELIX ("narrow pelvis")
Group: ornithischians, marginocephalians, pachycephalosaurs
Period: Early Cretaceous
Size and weight: 1.5m (5ft) long, 20kg (44lb)
Location: Germany
Description: Herbivore with broad hips, a stiff tail and short arms. It walked on two legs. Its skull has not been found.

STOKESOSAURUS ("Stokes' lizard")
Group: saurischians, theropods, coelurosaurs
Period: Late Jurassic
Size and weight: 4m (13ft) long, 80kg (175lb)
Location: USA
Description: Predator with a blunt snout. It walked on two legs and was probably a primitive tyrannosaur.

STRUTHIOMIMUS ("ostrich mimic")
Group: saurischians, theropods, coelurosaurs
Period: Late Cretaceous
Size and weight: 4m (13ft) long, 160kg (355lb)
Location: Canada
Description: Fast-running omnivore with three fingers on each hand. It had a toothless beak, long neck and long, slim arms. Its shins were longer than its thighs and it walked on two legs.

STRUTHIOSAURUS ("ostrich lizard")
Group: ornithischians, thyreophorans, ankylosaurs
Period: Late Cretaceous
Size and weight: 2m (7ft) long, 40kg (88lb)
Location: eastern Europe
Description: A plated herbivore with spikes on its neck, back and tail. It walked on four legs. Not much is known about it.

STYGIMOLOCH ("Hell Creek demon")
Group: ornithischians, marginocephalians, pachycephalosaurs
Period: Late Cretaceous
Size and weight: 2m (7ft) long, 35kg (77lb)
Location: USA
Description: Herbivore with a beak, a wide body and spikes on its dome-shaped skull. It walked on two legs.

STYRACOSAURUS ("spiked lizard")
Group: ornithischians, marginocephalans, ceratopsians
Period: Late Cretaceous
Size and weight: 5.5m (18ft) long, 900kg (1,985lb)
Location: Canada
Description: Herbivore with a large, upward-pointing nose horn and long spikes around the edges of its neck frill. It had a toothless beak and it walked on four legs.

SUCHOMIMUS ("crocodile mimic")
Group: saurischians, theropods, spinosaurs
Period: Early Cretaceous
Size and weight: 11m (36ft) long, 3.8 tonnes (4.2 tons)
Location: northern Africa
Description: Large predator with large thumb claws. It had an extremely long skull that was shaped like a crocodile's skull, and a ridge along its back. It walked on two legs.

SUPERSAURUS ("super lizard")
Group: saurischians, sauropodomorphs, sauropods
Period: Late Jurassic
Size and weight: 45m (148ft) long, 50 tonnes (55 tons)
Location: USA
Description: Giant, long-necked herbivore with pencil-shaped teeth and a long tail. It walked on four legs.

SYNTARSUS ("fused tarsus")
Group: saurischians, theropods, coelophysoids
Period: Early Jurassic
Size and weight: 2m (7ft) long, 15kg (33lb)
Location: southern Africa, USA and Wales
Description: Predator with a narrow skull, a long tail, and teeth suitable for catching both small and large prey. It had two small crests on its head, similar to those on Dilophosaurus.

SZECHUANOSAURUS ("Sichuan lizard")
Group: saurischians, theropods, allosaurs
Period: Late Jurassic
Size and weight: 4m (13ft), 130kg (290lb)
Location: China
Description: Predator that might have been similar to Sinraptor. It walked on two legs.

TALARURUS ("wicker tail")
Group: ornithischians, thyreophorans, ankylosaurs
Period: Late Cretaceous
Size and weight: 5m (16ft) long, 700kg (1,545lb)
Location: Mongolia
Description: Plated herbivore with a narrow skull, a beak, small teeth and a club at the end of its tail. It walked on four legs.

TANGVAYOSAURUS ("Tang Vay lizard")
Group: saurischians, sauropodomorphs, sauropods
Period: Early Cretaceous
Size and weight: 15m (49ft) long, 13 tonnes (14 tons)
Location: Laos
Description: A primitive titanosaur. It was a herbivore with a long neck and sturdy, column-like legs. It walked on four legs.

TANIUS ("for Tan")
Group: ornithischians, ornithopods, iguanodonts
Period: Late Cretaceous
Size and weight: 6m (20ft) long, 1.5 tonnes (1.7 tons)
Location: China
Description: Herbivore with a beak shaped like a duck's beak, and grinding teeth. It had a flat head and could walk on two or four legs.

TARASCOSAURUS ("Tarasque lizard")
Group: saurischians, theropods, neoceratosaurs
Period: Late Cretaceous
Size and weight: 5.5m (18ft) long, 370kg (815lb)
Location: France
Description: Predator that might have been similar to Carnotaurus. It walked on two legs. Not much is known about it.

TARBOSAURUS ("terrible lizard")
Group: saurischians, theropods, coelurosaurs
Period: Late Cretaceous
Size and weight: 10m (33ft) long, 5 tonnes (5.5 tons)
Location: Mongolia
Description: Giant predator with small arms, two fingers on each hand and a very large skull. It walked on two powerful legs. Tarbosaurus is the largest-known Asian predator. It might be the same animal as Tyrannosaurus.

TARCHIA ("brainy one")
Group: ornithischians, thyreophorans, ankylosaurs
Period: Late Cretaceous
Size and weight: 8m (26ft) long, 2.3 tonnes (2.5 tons)
Location: Mongolia
Description: Plated herbivore with a wide beak, short legs and a tail club. It walked on four legs.

TATISAURUS ("Ta-ti lizard")
Group: ornithischians, thyreophorans, ankylosaurs
Period: Early Jurassic
Size and weight: 1.5m (5ft) long, 20kg (44lb)
Location: China
Description: Small herbivore, perhaps the same animal as Scelidosaurus. It walked on four legs.

TAVEIROSAURUS ("Taveiro lizard")
Group: ornithischians, possibly thyreophorans, and possibly ankylosaurs
Period: Late Cretaceous
Size and weight: 90cm (35in) long, 5kg (11lb)
Location: Portugal, Spain and France
Description: Small herbivore known only from its teeth. It might have been a plated dinosaur and might have walked on four legs.

TECHNOSAURUS ("Texas Tech lizard")
Group: ornithischians
Period: Late Triassic
Size and weight: 1m (3ft) long, 4kg (8.8lb)
Location: USA
Description: Small herbivore with long, slim back legs, short arms and a beak. It walked on two legs.

TECOVASAURUS ("Tecovas lizard")
Group: ornithischians
Period: Late Jurassic
Size and weight: 1m (3ft) long, 4kg (8.8lb)
Location: USA
Description: Dinosaur known only from its teeth. It was either a herbivore or an omnivore and it walked on two legs. It might have been similar to Lesothosaurus.

TEHUELCHESAURUS ("Tehuelche lizard")
Group: saurischians, sauropodomorphs, sauropods
Period: Middle Jurassic
Size and weight: 15m (49ft) long, 7 tonnes (7.7 tons)
Location: Argentina
Description: Long-necked herbivore with sturdy, column-like legs. It walked on four legs.

TELMATOSAURUS ("swamp lizard")
Group: ornithischians, ornithopods, iguanodonts
Period: Late Cretaceous
Size and weight: 5m (16ft) long, 1 tonne (1.1 tons)
Location: Romania, France and Spain
Description: Primitive hadrosaur. It was a herbivore with a beak shaped like a duck's beak. It could walk on two or four legs.

TENDAGURIA ("for Tendaguru")
Group: saurischians, sauropodomorphs, sauropods
Period: Late Jurassic
Size and weight: 20m (66ft) long, 15 tonnes (17 tons)
Location: eastern Africa
Description: Large, long-necked herbivore known only from bones in its back. It walked on four legs.

TENONTOSAURUS ("tendon lizard")
Group: ornithischians, ornithopods, iguanodonts
Period: Early Cretaceous
Size and weight: 4.5m (15ft) long, 240kg (530lb)
Location: USA
Description: Primitive iguanodont with an extremely long tail. It was a herbivore with a beak, large eyes and five fingers on each hand. It walked on four legs.

TEXASETES ("Texas dweller")
Group: ornithischians, thyreophorans, ankylosaurs
Period: Early Cretaceous
Size and weight: 5m (16ft) long, 700kg (1,545lb)
Location: USA
Description: Herbivore with hard plates covering its neck, back and tail. It walked on four legs.

TEYUWASU ("big lizard")
Group: saurischians, and possibly theropods
Period: Late Triassic
Size and weight: 3m (10ft) long, 20kg (44lb)
Location: Brazil
Description: Predator known only from its leg bones. It might have been similar to Coelophysis and it walked on two legs.

THECODONTOSAURUS ("socket-toothed lizard")
Group: saurischians, sauropodomorphs
Period: Late Triassic
Size and weight: 2.5m (8ft) long, 24kg (53lb)
Location: England and Wales
Description: Dinosaur with leaf-shaped teeth, a blunt skull and a long tail. It had a short neck compared to other sauropodomorphs. It was an omnivore and walked on two legs.

THERIZINOSAURUS ("reaping lizard")
Group: saurischians, theropods, coelurosaurs
Period: Late Cretaceous
Size and weight: 10m (33ft) long, 6 tonnes (6.6 tons)
Location: Mongolia
Description: Large, long-necked herbivore with tiny, leaf-shaped teeth. It had long arms and enormous claws on its hands. Its claws were longer than any other dinosaur's. It walked on two legs.

THESCELOSAURUS ("surprising lizard")
Group: ornithischians, ornithopods, and possibly hypsilophodontids
Period: Late Cretaceous
Size and weight: 3.5m (11ft) long, 60kg (130lb)
Location: USA and Canada
Description: Herbivore with a beak, a bulky body and a stiff tail. It had short hands with five fingers on each hand. It walked on two legs.

TIANCHIASAURUS ("Heavenly Pool lizard")
Group: ornithischians, thyreophorans, ankylosaurs
Period: Middle Jurassic
Size and weight: 5m (16ft) long, 700kg (1,545lb)
Location: China
Description: Herbivore with plates covering its neck, back and tail. It had short legs and a wide body. It walked on four legs.

TIANZHENOSAURUS ("Tianzhen lizard")
Group: ornithischians, thyreophorans, ankylosaurs
Period: Late Cretaceous
Size and weight: 3m (10ft) long, 70kg (155lb)
Location: China
Description: Herbivore with a wide, horned skull. Its neck, back and tail were covered in plates. It walked on four legs.

TIENSHANOSAURUS ("Heavenly Mountains lizard")
Group: saurischians, sauropodomorphs, sauropods
Period: Late Jurassic
Size and weight: 10m (33ft) long, 8 tonnes (8.8 tons)
Location: China
Description: Herbivore with a long neck and tail, a large body and slim, column-like legs. It was small compared to other sauropods and walked on four legs.

TIMIMUS ("Tim's ornithomimid")
Group: saurischians, theropods, coelurosaurs
Period: Early Cretaceous
Size and weight: 3m (10ft) long, 130kg (290lb)
Location: Australia
Description: Dinosaur known only from one leg bone. It might have been similar to Ornithomimus and it was either a herbivore or an omnivore. It walked on two legs.

TITANOSAURUS ("Titan lizard")
Group: saurischians, sauropodomorphs, sauropods
Period: Late Cretaceous
Size and weight: 18m (59ft) long, 11 tonnes (12 tons)
Location: India, Spain and Argentina
Description: Large, long-necked herbivore with column-like legs, a heavy body and a small head. It had protective plates on its back and walked on four legs.

TOCHISAURUS ("ostrich lizard")
Group: saurischians, theropods, coelurosaurs
Period: Late Cretaceous
Size and weight: 1m (3ft) long, 5kg (11lb)
Location: China
Description: Predator with long, slim hind legs and raised second toes. It was small and walked on two legs. Not much is known about it.

TOROSAURUS ("perforated lizard")
Group: ornithischians, marginocephalians, ceratopsians
Period: Late Cretaceous
Size and weight: 7.6m (25ft) long, 2.7 tonnes (3 tons)
Location: USA
Description: Giant ceratopsian with an enormous skull that made up half the length of its body (not including its tail). It had a beak, a neck frill and three horns on its face. It was a herbivore and walked on four legs.

TORVOSAURUS ("savage lizard")
Group: saurischians, theropods, spinosaurs
Period: Late Jurassic
Size and weight: 9m (30ft) long, 2 tonnes (2.2 tons)
Location: USA
Description: Predator with strong, short arms, powerful legs and sharp, backward-curving teeth. It walked on two legs.

TRICERATOPS ("three horned face")
Group: ornithischians, marginocephalians, ceratopsians
Period: Late Cretaceous
Size and weight: 8m (26ft) long, 3 tonnes (3.3 tons)
Location: USA and Canada
Description: Herbivore with three horns on its face, a neck frill and a prominent beak, like a parrot's beak. It was the largest ceratopsian and walked on four legs.

TRIMUCRODON ("triple-point tooth")
Group: ornithischians, and probably heterodontosaurids
Period: Late Jurassic
Size and weight: 1m (3ft) long, 5kg (11lb)
Location: Portugal
Description: Small herbivore known only from its teeth. It might have been similar to Heterodontosaurus.

TROODON ("wounding tooth")
Group: saurischians, theropods, coelurosaurs
Period: Late Cretaceous
Size and weight: 3m (10ft) long, 45kg (100lb)
Location: USA and Canada
Description: Long-legged predator that was either a carnivore or an omnivore. It walked on two legs and had a slim skull and raised second toes. It had sharp teeth and long, slim jaws.

TSAGANTEGIA ("from Tsagan-Teg")
Group: ornithischians, thyreophorans, ankylosaurs
Period: Late Cretaceous
Size and weight: 6m (20ft) long, 1.3 tonnes (1.4 tons)
Location: Mongolia
Description: Plated herbivore with a box-shaped skull, a narrow beak and small teeth. It walked on four legs.

TSINTAOSAURUS ("Qingdao lizard")
Group: ornithischians, ornithopods, iguanodonts
Period: Late Cretaceous
Size and weight: 9m (30ft) long, 4.5 tonnes (5 tons)
Location: China
Description: Herbivore with a forward-pointing head crest in the shape of a spike. It had a beak shaped like a duck's beak, and grinding teeth. It could walk on two or four legs.

TUOJIANGOSAURUS ("Tuo River lizard")
Group: ornithischians, thyreophorans, stegosaurs
Period: Late Jurassic
Size and weight: 7m (23ft) long, 2.5 tonnes (2.8 tons)
Location: China
Description: Herbivore with plates along its neck, back and tail, and two pairs of spikes on its tail. It had a small, low head and a toothless beak. It walked on four legs.

TURANOCERATOPS ("Turanian horned face")
Group: ornithischians, marginocephalians, ceratopsians
Period: Late Cretaceous
Size and weight: 5m (16ft) long, 1 tonne (1.1 tons)
Location: Uzbekistan
Description: Herbivore with a beak, a neck frill and horns above its eyes. It walked on four legs.

TYLOCEPHALE ("swelling head")
Group: ornithischians, marginocephalians, pachycephalosaurs
Period: Late Cretaceous
Size and weight: 2.5m (8ft) long, 52kg (115lb)
Location: Mongolia
Description: Thick-skulled herbivore that walked on two legs.

TYRANNOSAURUS ("tyrant lizard")
Group: saurischians, theropods, coelurosaurs
Period: Late Cretaceous
Size and weight: 11m (36ft) long, 6 tonnes (6.6 tons)
Location: USA and Canada
Description: Large predator with short arms and small hands, with two fingers on each hand. It had a huge skull, powerful jaws and sharp teeth. It walked on two legs.

UDANOCERATOPS ("Udan horned face")
Group: ornithischians, marginocephalians, ceratopsians
Period: Late Cretaceous
Size and weight: 4m (13ft) long, 750kg (1,655lb)
Location: Mongolia
Description: Herbivore with a beak, a neck frill and a narrow snout. It walked on four legs.

UNENLAGIA ("half bird")
Group: saurischians, theropods
Period: Late Cretaceous
Size and weight: 3m (10ft) long, 50kg (110lb)
Location: Argentina
Description: Bird-like predator with long arms. It walked on two legs and might have been similar to Deinonychus.

UNQUILLOSAURUS ("Unquillo lizard")
Group: saurischians, theropods, and possibly coelurosaurs
Period: Late Cretaceous
Size and weight: 6m (20ft) long, 700kg (1,545lb)
Location: Argentina
Description: Large predator known only from one pelvic bone. It walked on two legs.

UTAHRAPTOR ("Utah thief")
Group: saurischians, theropods, coelurosaurs
Period: Early Cretaceous
Size and weight: 7m (23ft) long, 450kg (990lb)
Location: USA
Description: Big predator with large curved claws on each second toe. It walked on two legs.

VALDORAPTOR ("Wealden thief")
Group: saurischians, theropods, allosaurs
Period: Early Cretaceous
Size and weight: 6m (20ft) long, 700kg (1,545lb)
Location: England
Description: Predator known only from its foot bones. It walked on two legs and might have been similar to Neovenator.

VALDOSAURUS ("Wealden lizard")
Group: ornithischians, ornithopods, iguanodonts
Period: Early Cretaceous
Size and weight: 4m (13ft) long, 140kg (310lb)
Location: England, Romania and northern Africa
Description: Herbivore with short arms, three toes on each foot and a toothless beak. It walked on two legs.

VARIRAPTOR ("Var thief")
Group: saurischians, theropods, coelurosaurs
Period: Late Cretaceous
Size and weight: 2m (7ft) long, 15kg (33lb)
Location: France
Description: Bird-like predator with long arms and large foot claws. It walked on two legs.

VELOCIRAPTOR ("swift thief")
Group: saurischians, theropods, coelurosaurs
Period: Late Cretaceous
Size and weight: 2m (7ft) long, 15kg (33lb)
Location: Mongolia
Description: Bird-like predator with long arms. It walked on two legs and had long claws on its second toes.

VELOCISAURUS ("swift lizard")
Group: saurischians, theropods, neoceratosaurs
Period: Late Cretaceous
Size and weight: 1.5m (5ft) long, 8kg (18lb)
Location: Argentina
Description: Small predator with long, slim, hind legs. It probably had short arms and it walked on two legs.

VENENOSAURUS ("poison lizard")
Group: saurischians, sauropodomorphs, sauropods
Period: Early Cretaceous
Size and weight: 13m (43ft) long, 7 tonnes (7.7 tons)
Location: USA
Description: Long-necked herbivore with a short tail and long front legs. It walked on four legs.

VOLKHEIMERIA ("for Volkheimer")
Group: saurischians, sauropodomorphs, sauropods
Period: Middle Jurassic
Size and weight: 16m (53ft) long, 20 tonnes (22 tons)
Location: Argentina
Description: Long-necked herbivore that might have been similar to Brachiosaurus. It walked on four legs.

VULCANODON ("volcano tooth")
Group: saurischians, sauropodomorphs, sauropods
Period: Early Jurassic
Size and weight: 6.5m (21ft) long, 2 tonnes (2.2 tons)
Location: southern Africa
Description: Long-necked herbivore with knees and ankles that were more flexible than those of later sauropods. It walked on four legs.

WAKINOSAURUS ("Wakino lizard")
Group: theropods, and possibly allosaurs
Period: Early Cretaceous
Size and weight: unknown
Location: Japan
Description: Carnivorous dinosaur known only from a single tooth.

WANNANOSAURUS ("southern Wan lizard")
Group: ornithischians, marginocephalians, pachycephalosaurs
Period: Late Cretaceous
Size and weight: 1m (3ft) long, 9kg (20lb)
Location: China
Description: Herbivore with a beak and a broad body. The top of its skull was thick and flat.

WUERHOSAURUS ("Wuerho lizard")
Group: ornithischians, thyreophorans, stegosaurs
Period: Early Cretaceous
Size and weight: 4.5m (15ft) long, 650kg (1,430lb)
Location: China
Description: Herbivore with plates sticking up along its neck, back and tail. It walked on four legs.

XENOTARSOSAURUS ("strange tarsus lizard")
Group: saurischians, theropods, neoceratosaurs
Period: Late Cretaceous
Size and weight: 5.5m (18ft) long, 370kg (815lb)
Location: Argentina
Description: Large, long-legged predator that probably had short arms. It walked on two legs.

XUANHANOSAURUS ("Xuanhan lizard")
Group: saurischians, theropods, and possibly spinosaurs
Period: Middle Jurassic
Size and weight: 6m (20ft) long, 700kg (1,545lb)
Location: China
Description: Medium-sized predator that walked on two legs and had a stiff tail. It is thought to have had longer and more powerful arms than other spinosaurs.

YANDUSAURUS ("Salt Capital lizard")
Group: ornithischians, ornithopods, hypsilophodontids
Period: Middle Jurassic
Size and weight: 1.5m (5ft) long, 10kg (22lb)
Location: China
Description: Small herbivore with a short skull, large eyes and a narrow beak. It walked on two legs.

YANGCHUANOSAURUS ("Yangchuan lizard")
Group: saurischians, theropods, allosaurs
Period: Late Jurassic
Size and weight: 10m (33ft) long, 3.5 tonnes (3.9 tons)
Location: China
Description: Large predator with ridges and horns on its head. It walked on two legs.

YAVERLANDIA ("from Yaverland")
Group: ornithischians, marginocephalians, pachycephalosaurs
Period: Early Cretaceous
Size and weight: 90cm (35in) long, 7kg (15lb)
Location: England
Description: An early pachycephalosaur known only from the top of its thick, flat skull. It was small, walked on two legs and was a herbivore.

YIMENOSAURUS ("Yimen lizard")
Group: saurischians, sauropodomorphs, prosauropods
Period: Early Jurassic
Size and weight: 9m (30ft) long, 3 tonnes (3.3 tons)
Location: China
Description: Long-necked herbivore with a short skull and spoon-shaped teeth. It could walk on two or four legs.

YUNNANOSAURUS ("Yunnan lizard")
Group: saurischians, sauropodomorphs, prosauropods
Period: Early Jurassic
Size and weight: 7m (23ft) long, 1 tonne (1.1 tons)
Location: China
Description: Long-necked herbivore with a sturdy body and a sloping snout. It walked on four legs.

ZEPHYROSAURUS ("Zephyr's lizard")
Group: ornithischians, ornithopods, hypsilophodontids
Period: Early Cretaceous
Size and weight: 1.8m (6ft) long, 15kg (33lb)
Location: USA
Description: Long-necked herbivore with long hind legs and short arms. It had a short skull and large eyes, and it walked on two legs.

ZIZHONGOSAURUS ("Zizhong lizard")
Group: saurischians, sauropodomorphs, sauropods
Period: Early Jurassic
Size and weight: 9m (30ft) long, 450kg (990lb)
Location: China
Description: A small, primitive sauropod. It had a long neck, a bulky body and long front legs. It walked on four legs and was a herbivore.

ZUNICERATOPS ("Zuni horned face")
Group: ornithischians, marginocephalians, ceratopsians
Period: Late Cretaceous
Size and weight: 4m (13ft) long, 750kg (1,655lb)
Location: USA
Description: Primitive ceratopsian with a large neck frill and long horns above its eyes. It walked on four legs and was a herbivore.

Glossary

This glossary explains some of the words you may come across while reading about dinosaurs. Words in italics have their own entry elsewhere in the glossary.

abelisaurs A group of *theropod* dinosaurs, known from India and South America. Some abelisaurs had stout horns on their heads.

adaptation The way a plant or animal *species* develops over time to suit its environment.

allosaurs A group of *theropod* dinosaurs. Allosaurs first appeared in the *Jurassic period* and died out before the end of the *Cretaceous period*. Many allosaurs had horns or ridges on their heads.

amphibians A group of soft-skinned animals that live both on land and in water. For example, frogs are a kind of amphibian.

ankylosaurs A group of *ornithischian* dinosaurs that walked on four legs. They were *herbivores* and their bodies were covered in protective bony plates and spikes.

Antarctic Circle An imaginary line that runs parallel to the *Equator*. The area south of the line is known as the Antarctic and includes the South Pole.

archosaurs A group of reptiles that includes dinosaurs and *pterosaurs*. The first archosaurs were crocodile-like animals that first appeared around 250 million years ago.

asteroid A large chunk of rock and metal in space. Occasionally, asteroids collide with Earth. Scientists think this may have happened at the end of the *Cretaceous period*, causing the *extinction* of the dinosaurs.

atmosphere A layer of gases that surrounds a planet or star. Earth has an atmosphere.

avian dinosaur Another name for a bird. Birds are descended from dinosaurs. Scientifically speaking, this means birds are, in fact, a type of dinosaur.

badland An area of bare, rocky land that is continually eroded by wind and rain.

body fossil A *fossil* of any of the hard parts of an animal, such as the bones or teeth.

brachiosaurs A group of extremely tall *sauropod* dinosaurs that had front legs longer than their back legs.

carcharodontosaurs A group of large *theropod* dinosaurs known from Africa and South America.

carnivore An animal that only eats meat.

ceratopsians A group of *ornithischian* dinosaurs. Most ceratopsians walked on four legs and had bony frills at the back of their skulls, and horns on their faces. They were *herbivores*.

climate The typical weather conditions in a particular region.

clone To make an exact copy of an animal using its *DNA*.

coelophysoids A group of small to medium-sized *theropod* dinosaurs. Coelophysoids lived in the early part of the *Mesozoic era*.

coelurosaurs A group of *theropod* dinosaurs that are closely related to birds.

continent One of the Earth's major land masses.

coprolite A piece of fossilized dung.

crater A hollow made by the impact of a space rock, such as an *asteroid*.

crest A horn-like ridge on the top of an animal's head.

Cretaceous period A period of time lasting from 144 to 65 million years ago. Dinosaurs, and many other animal groups, died out at the end of the Cretaceous period.

crust The Earth's solid outer layer, which together with the upper part of the *mantle*, is made up of *plates*.

diagnostic bone A bone that *paleontologists* can use to identify an animal. Diagnostic bones are unique to a particular *species* of animal.

DNA (deoxyribonucleic acid) A very complex chemical found in every living thing. DNA contains a huge amount of information about how living things function.

dromaeosaurs A fierce group of *theropod* dinosaurs with especially long, sharp claws. Dromaeosaurs are very closely related to birds.

Equator An imaginary line around the middle of the Earth, exactly halfway between the poles.

erosion The wearing away of rocks and soil by seas and rivers, the weather, and the actions of plants and animals.

evolution The development of a *species* over time as it adapts to its environment. The development takes place very gradually through a series of small changes.

excavation The removal of buried objects by digging.

extinction The death of an entire *species* of animals or plants. This usually happens very gradually, over millions of years.

fault A crack in the Earth's *crust*.

flapping flight Powered flight achieved by flapping wings rather than by gliding.

flash flood A sudden, violent flood that usually takes place after heavy rain.

fold mountains A mountain range formed by the Earth's *crust* buckling up when *plates* push together.

fossil The remains or trace of a plant or animal preserved in rock.

geologist Someone who studies the structure of the Earth and what it is made of.

Gondwana A huge *continent* that covered the southern part of the world during the *Jurassic period*. The modern continents that made up Gondwana are South America, Africa, India, Australia and Antarctica.

hadrosaurs A group of *ornithopod* dinosaurs. Hadrosaurs were *herbivores* and were very common during the *Cretaceous period*. Many hadrosaurs had *crests* on their heads.

herbivore An animal that only eats plants.

herd A group of animals that lives and feeds together.

heterodontosaurids A group of small *ornithischian* dinosaurs that lived from the early *Jurassic* to the early *Cretaceous period*.

hoodoo A natural rock formation shaped by wind and rain.

horned dinosaur Another term for a *ceratopsian* dinosaur, as ceratopsians had horns on their faces.

hypsilophodontids A group of small *ornithopod* dinosaurs.

ichthyosaurs Sea reptiles that lived during the *Mesozoic era*.

iguanodontids A group of *ornithopod* dinosaurs that ate plants. Many iguanodontids had a sharp spike on each thumb.

Jurassic period A period of time lasting from 208 to 144 million years ago.

K–T boundary The time between the end of the *Cretaceous period*, 65 million years ago, and the beginning of the *Tertiary period*. It was during this time that many animal groups, including dinosaurs, became extinct.

land bridge A land link between *two continents*.

Laurasia The huge *continent* that covered the northern part of the world during the *Jurassic period*. The modern continents that make up Laurasia are North America, Europe and Asia.

lava Hot rock that bursts or flows out of volcanoes.

magma Hot, molten rock inside the Earth.

maniraptorans A group of *theropods* that includes *dromaeosaurs* and birds. Maniraptorans are characterized by a small bone in their wrists that is shaped like a half-moon.

mantle The thick layer of rock beneath the Earth's *crust*. Some of it is solid and some of it is molten (melted).

marginocephalians A group of *ornithischian* dinosaurs that had a bony shelf at the back of their skulls.

marine rock *Sedimentary rock* that formed under seas or oceans.

Mesozoic era A period of time lasting from 250 to 65 million years ago. It is divided up into the *Triassic, Jurassic* and *Cretaceous periods*.

migration Moving from one place to another at certain times of the year, for example to search for food or warmer weather.

mummification The preservation of the soft parts of a dead animal, such as the skin and the organs.

natural selection The survival of plants or animals with qualities that suit their environment. Those qualities are then passed on to their offspring.

neoceratosaurs A group of *theropod* dinosaurs. Most were medium to large *predators*, with four fingers on each hand. Many neoceratosaurs had horns on their heads.

omnivore An animal that eats both meat and plants.

ornithischians One of the two main groups into which dinosaurs are divided. Ornithischian dinosaurs had hipbones similar to modern birds' hipbones.

ornithomimosaurs A group of plant-eating *theropod* dinosaurs with long, powerful hind legs. Ornithomimosaurs were probably the fastest dinosaurs.

ornithopods A major group of *ornithischian* dinosaurs that walked either on two or four legs. All ornithopods were herbivores and had beaks.

oviraptors A group of bird-like *theropod* dinosaurs. Oviraptors were covered in feathers and had beaks. They lived during the *Cretaceous period*.

pachycephalosaurs A group of *ornithischian* dinosaurs with thick skulls. Pachycephalosaurs were *herbivores* and walked on two legs.

pachypleurosaurs A group of small, lizard-like marine reptiles with small heads, long necks, paddle-like limbs and webbed feet. They first appeared in the mid-Triassic period and died out at the end of the *Triassic period*.

paleontologist Someone who studies *fossils*.

Pangaea The huge *continent* that existed at the beginning of the *Mesozoic era*. It gradually broke up to form the continents we have today.

Panthalassa Ocean The huge ocean that covered two-thirds of the Earth's surface at the beginning of the *Mesozoic era*.

plate One of the huge pieces of rock that make up the Earth's surface. Plates are made up of the Earth's *crust* and the upper part of the *mantle*.

plesiosaurs A group of reptiles that lived in the seas and oceans during the *Mesozoic era*. They had short tails and four flippers. There were two main kinds – long-necked plesiosaurs, and short-necked plesiosaurs, known as *pliosaurs*.

pliosaurs A type of *plesiosaur*. Pliosaurs had short necks, huge heads and powerful jaws and teeth. They lived during the *Cretaceous period*.

predator An animal that hunts other animals for food.

prehistoric animal An animal that lived before people existed.

prey An animal hunted by other animals for food.

primitive animal An early form of a particular type of animal. They lack some of the features seen in later animals from the same group.

prosauropods A group of mostly plant-eating *saurischian* dinosaurs with long necks and tails. Prosauropods are among the earliest-known dinosaurs. They are very similar to *sauropods*, but did not grow as large.

pterosaurs Flying reptiles that lived during the *Mesozoic era*.

quarry A place where stones or *fossils* are excavated from the ground.

resin A thick, sticky liquid that comes from plants and trees. It is usually clear, yellow or brownish.

ribcage The cage-like structure of bones that protects the internal organs.

rift valley A valley that is formed when two *plates* move apart. The chunk of *crust* between them collapses to form a deep, wide valley.

sand dune Sand that has been blown into a mound or ridge by the wind.

satellite image An image taken from space.

saurischians One of the two main groups into which dinosaurs are divided. Saurischian dinosaurs had hipbones that were similar in shape to modern lizards' hipbones.

sauropodomorphs A group of mostly plant-eating *saurischian* dinosaurs that walked on four legs and had long necks and tails. Sauropodomorphs are further divided into *prosauropods* and *sauropods*.

sauropods A group of plant-eating *saurischian* dinosaurs with long necks and tails. Sauropods are the largest ever land animals.

scrubland Land covered with small trees, bushes or shrubs.

sediment Fragments of mud or sand.

sedimentary rock Rock made up of fragments of mud and sand. Sedimentary rock is formed when fragments settle on a seabed or a riverbed and are gradually squashed down to form hard rock.

species A type of plant, animal or other living thing.

spinosaurs A group of *theropod* dinosaurs. Some spinosaurs ate fish.

stegosaurs A group of *ornithischian* dinosaurs that

walked on four legs. They were *herbivores* and had bony plates sticking up from their neck, back and tail. Some stegosaurs also had spikes on their tail and shoulders.

Tertiary period A period of time that lasted from 66 to 1.8 million years ago. The Tertiary period followed the *Cretaceous period*.

Tethys Ocean The ocean that covered the area where the Mediterranean Sea is today, during the *Mesozoic era*.

therizinosaurs A group of plant-eating *theropod* dinosaurs known from Asia and North America. Therizinosaurs had feathers on their bodies and huge claws on their hands.

theropods A group of *saurischian* dinosaurs that walked on two legs. Most theropods were *carnivores*.

thyreophorans A group of *ornithischian* dinosaurs that includes *stegosaurs* and *ankylosaurs*. Thyreophorans walked on four legs and had bony plates or spikes on their bodies.

titanosaurs A group of *sauropod* dinosaurs that had bony lumps of skin on their bodies.

trace fossil A fossilized track or imprint left behind by an animal or plant.

trackway A series of dinosaur footprints found together.

trench A deep valley in the seabed that forms where one *plate* is forced under another.

Triassic period A period of time that lasted from 250 to 208 million years ago.

tyrannosaurs A group of *theropod* dinosaurs that lived during the *Cretaceous period*. Most tyrannosaurs were huge, with large teeth, long legs and tiny arms.

Wealden rock Rock from a region of southeast England.

x-rays Rays that are able to go through solid substances. X-rays can be used to create images that show what's inside objects.

Answers to dinosaur quiz (pages 116–117)

Picture round

1. a. theropod
2. c. theropod
3. b. dromaeosaur
4. b. Cretaceous

Survival challenge

1. a. Ceratopsians are plant-eaters, so will not attack you,

whereas Albertosaurus is a deadly predator.

2. a. Run away. You are the fastest dinosaur, so Tarbosaurus has little hope of catching you.

3. b. Stay where you are. As a small dinosaur, you do not have the energy to make a long journey to a warmer area.

4. a. Rejoin the safety of the herd. Even though you are such a large dinosaur, Allosaurus is still

capable of attacking you while you are on your own, but is unlikely to approach a herd.

Quick quiz

1. herbivores
2. Antarctica
3. North America
4. Microraptor
5. paleontologists
6. China
7. hadrosaurs
8. At the end of the Cretaceous period, 65 million years ago.

Index

Acknowledgements

Every effort has been made to trace the copyright holders of the material in this book. If any rights have been omitted, the publishers offer to rectify this in any subsequent editions following notification. The publishers are grateful to the following organizations and individuals for their permission to reproduce material (t=top, m=middle, b=bottom, l=left, r=right):

Cover © François Gohier/Ardea London; **p1** © Richard T. Nowitz/CORBIS; **p2** © François Gohier/Ardea London; **p10–11** © Pat Canova/Index Stock Imagery; **p14–15** © François Gohier/Ardea London; **p15** (br) P. J. Green/Ardea London; **p16** (b) Specimen courtesy Gaston Design. Photo © François Gohier/Ardea London; **p16–17** © Sue Clark/Alamy; **p17** (tl) © François Gohier/Ardea London; **p18–19** © Dutheil Didier/CORBIS SYGMA; **p19** (tr) © Layne Kennedy/CORBIS; **p20** © AP Photo/Siddiqi Ray; **p21** © O. LOUIS MAZZATENTA National Geographic Image Collection; **p20-21** (background) © Digital Vision; **p22** © The Natural History Museum, London; **p23** (t) © The Natural History Museum, London, (br) © Witmer/Parsons; **p22–23** (background) © Digital Vision; **p24** Courtesy of Universal Studios Licensing, LLLP THE KOBAL COLLECTION/AMBLIN/UNIVERSAL, (mr) © MC LEOD MURDO/CORBIS SYGMA; **p25** (t) © François Gohier/Ardea London, (b) © Tim Flannery; **p26–27** © Francesco Reginato/The Image Bank; **p28–29** © Galen Rowell/CORBIS; **p29** (b) © The Natural History Museum, London; **p30–31** (background) © Digital Vision; **p38** © Kevin Schafer/CORBIS; **p39** (tr) © Kennan Ward Photography/CORBIS, (b) © François Gohier/Ardea London; **p40–41** © CORBIS; **p41** (tr) © Sanford/Agliolo/CORBIS; **p42** (t) © Roger Ressmeyer/CORBIS; **p43** © Martin Harvey; Gallo Images/CORBIS; **p44** © The Natural History Museum, London; **p45** (br) © J. J. Brooks/Aquila; **p46–47** © Scott T. Smith/CORBIS; **p48** © François Gohier/Ardea London; **p49** (m) Images by Barbara Summey, NASA GSFC Visualization Analysis Lab, based on Landsat 5 data provided by the Laboratory for Terrestrial Physics; **p52–53** © Hubert Stadler/CORBIS; **p53** © Andrew A. Skolnick, taken at the Field Museum, Chicago, (tr) © psihoyos.com; **p57** (t) © François Gohier/Ardea London; **p58** (m) © James L. Amos/CORBIS; **p58–59** © The Natural History Museum, London; **p60** (t) © Jan Butchofsky-Houser/CORBIS; **p61** (r) © The Natural History Museum, London; **p62** (mr) © François Gohier/Ardea London; **p63** (b) © Kevin Schafer/CORBIS; **p66–67** © O. Alamany & E. Vicens/CORBIS; **p71** (t) © PHOTOPRESS WASHINGTON/CORBIS SYGMA, (b) © 2000 Patricia Kane-Vanni; **p73** (br) © The Natural History Museum, London; **p75** (t&b) © The Natural History Museum, London; **p76–77** © Tom Bean/CORBIS; **p76** (br) © The Natural History Museum, London; **p78** (tr) © Nik Wheeler/CORBIS; **p82** (mr) © O. LOUIS MAZZATENTA National Geographic Image Collection; **p83** (l) © The Natural History Museum, London; **p84–85** © François Gohier/Ardea London; **p87** (t) © The Natural History Museum, London; **p90–91** © PETER MENZEL/SCIENCE PHOTO LIBRARY; **p93** (b) © William R. Hammer, Fritiof Fryxell Professor of Geology, Augustana College, Rock Island; **p95** (tl) © François Gohier/Ardea London; **p96** (t&b) © The Natural History Museum, London; **p97** (tr) © American Museum of Natural History; **p99** © François Gohier/Ardea London; **p100** © Nathan Benn/CORBIS; **p102–103** (background) © Digital Vision; **p104** (l) © DUTHEIL DIDIER/CORBIS SYGMA, (m) © AP Photo/Karen Tam; **p105** Willem J. Hillenius; **p106–107** © Jim Zuckerman/CORBIS; **p108** (tl) © The Geological Society/NHMPL, (m) © The Natural History Museum, London, (br) © Bettmann/CORBIS; **p108–109** © DUTHEIL DIDIER/CORBIS SYGMA; **p110** (l) © Gunter Marx Photography/CORBIS, (m) © The Natural History Museum, London, (br) © Bob Krist/CORBIS; **p111** © Bill Varie/CORBIS; **p114** © The Natural History Museum, London; **p115** (bl) © François Gohier/Ardea London, (tr) © Mike Hettwer, image provided by Project Exploration; **p114–115** (background) © Digital Vision; **p116** (bl) © Pat Morris/Ardea London, (m) © Tom Bean/CORBIS, (r) © 1998 Fossilworks, Inc. All Rights Reserved. **p118–135** (background) © Digital Vision.

Managing editor: Gillian Doherty
Managing designer: Mary Cartwright
Cover design by Zoë Wray.
Digital image processing by John Russell and Isaac Quaye.
Cartography by European Map Graphics Ltd. Small maps by Mike Olley. With thanks to Alice Pearcey.

Usborne Publishing is not responsible and does not accept liability for the availability or content of any website other than its own, or for any exposure to harmful, offensive, or inaccurate material which may appear on the Web. Usborne Publishing will have no liability for any damage or loss caused by viruses that may be downloaded as a result of browsing sites it recommends.